Under
the Broom Tree

Sean Caulfield

PAULIST PRESS
New York/Ramsey

Library of Congress
Catalog Card Number: 82-60593

ISBN: 0-8091-2493-9

Published by Paulist Press
545 Island Road, Ramsey, N.J. 07446

Printed and bound in the
United States of America

Contents

for four friends,

Nick,

and more

But (Elijah) himself went a day's journey into the wilderness, and came and sat down under a broom tree; and he asked that he might die, saying: "It is enough; now, O Lord, take away my life; for I am no better than my fathers." And he lay down and slept under a broom tree; and behold, an angel touched him, and said to him, "Arise and eat." And he looked and behold, there was at his head a cake baked on hot stones and a jar of water. And he ate and drank, and lay down again. And the angel of the Lord came again a second time, and touched him, and said, "Arise and eat, else the journey will be too great for you." And he arose, and ate and drank, and went in the strength of that food forty days and forty nights to Horeb, the mount of God.

1 Kings 4:4-8 (RVS)

Introduction

This is a story of that inner spiritual journey which accompanies transition. It is a story also of places and events, and of the friendly people who occasioned that journey in myself. But it is more than a story: it tells of the insights and reflections which emerge from such a journey, and of the doubts, fears, questioning and decision-making which are part of it.

Transition is that in-between time of faith and search, of prophetic discernment with regard to what is possible and what is not, of readapting to circumstances; that time when supreme good sense is required to re-establish an equilibrium when the outer forms of our lives have changed, and the inner depths have been stirred up. Such a change might be the death of a loved one, a disabling accident, a divorce, a move to new surroundings, the loss of employment, the loss of friends. Transition is a time of crisis in which, on the one hand, we are challenged to growth through confusion, decision and risk, while on the other hand we are tempted to the loss of everything by a refusal to accept that challenge. It is never a time of easy optimism.

In the broad outline, there are several steps we take which are common to all forms of transition. The first step is usually an extremely conservative reaction, a sort of defense mechanism. A young widower might swear fidelity to the memory of a young wife he has lost: "I'll never marry again." The disabled person feels that he will be a tragic figure for life. The laid-off employee will never take a job with the company again—he would rather starve than take a salary reduction. The woman who has lost a man-friend may say that she does not need men—"They're all a bunch of jerks anyway"—and that she can manage very well without them. One hears expressions such as "I'll never be hurt again" and "I've learned my lesson" which indicate withdrawal.

1

The second step follows the discovery that withdrawal never really works. One cannot live one's entire life in protest. The widower, to his embarrassment, discovers his inability to picture the face of his deceased in his imagination anymore. He has to pick up a snapshot to remind himself of her. He discovers that he is still in need of love, support and human affection. He begins to look around. The disabled person finds that people are short on sympathy for those who are long on self-pity. The unemployed person finds that beggars cannot be choosers, that hunger is a great teacher of wisdom, that preferring to starve may have been a noble sentiment considering the injustice, but that it was merely the mood of the moment. He begins to look for work. Life at its fullest will never come out of the defense of hurt feelings, out of negative reactions.

The third step is critical: still defensive, and yet having to make decisions about our lives, we are tempted to enthusiasms, to the making of any one of a number of unwise decisions. We need to be very aware of this. Our emotion, rather than our reason, is apt to be our guide, a blind guide. It is a time when we could profit from seeking advice, or from going through a discernment process. The trouble, however, is that at this time in our life we are more likely to close our ears in a stubborn manner to all the advice that is offered to us. The widower may look for a woman who will recreate in detail the qualities of his deceased love, wishing to relive his former life. That would be a very great mistake. The worker may dream of going into business for himself, or of doing a whole new line of work for which he has no talent whatever. The disabled person may insist that he can function in precisely the same manner as he did before the accident. During transition we are pulled in many directions, frequently overestimating what we are capable of doing.

If the transition is handled with honesty, with a minimum of brashness and self-vindication, the final step will be the recovery of a manner of life we are capable of living. It will be vastly more than that: it will be the end of a strange inner journey, and the discovery in greater depth of who we really are. We will perform the kind of work we know we can do. We will offer the gift we have, which is all anyone should try to offer. It will be a return to normalcy again, but as a deeper and more completely human person. There will be no desire to recreate in exact detail the former circumstances of our lives, but there will be no refusal of that life either. A widower may

2

acknowledge the need to lay all ghosts to rest and marry again. A person who lost a leg will learn to walk again. Disrupted relationships will be re-established on a new level. Life will go forward again, but the person will not be quite the same. It will have been a time of growth.

This book is not the work of a psychologist. It is not a textbook of abstract, or even practical, principles, though some of those are mentioned. It is largely an account of a flawed person's coping with God, life, change and love. Why bother to write about it? Because flawed people and clay feet are everywhere, and if one of us can put into words the experience of our inner journey, it will have elements which speak to all. Nor is real life an abstraction, neither is it guided by practical principles alone, there being a mystical element in every person's experience. One is never more fully human than when struggling through sheer nonsense about God, life, meaning and love. These are the absolutes which obsess us and always elude us. Nor does anyone know, quite in detail, what the principles are which should guide our decision-making in a time of transition. There are no final textbook answers: there is only life and its options. For that reason I rely on narrative more than theory to map this journey. Transition is personal, and so are our crises, but we've got to walk together.

My transition is not a tragedy, as is often the case in the transitions of others, yet it is keenly felt. It has several aspects. At the moment I am out of work—a time of ministry as chaplain to a community of religious women came abruptly to an end. I had to move on. This has left me feeling high and dry, in fact somewhat rejected. I feel incarcerated within my monastic enclosure, and useless, of no concern to God. His silence humiliates me. I find myself, also, separated by several hundred miles from a few very special friends. The deep relationship I have to my friends will underlie the whole of my spiritual journey. They have been a very positive force in my life. Their absence leaves me questioning the meaning of life and its purpose.

/Transition has more to do with what is happening within the spirit than with what is happening on the surface.\It will have to be a movement into a positive future, or life will become a meaningless drift.

3

1. Return to Start: Ritual

It is safe to say that since we are human, there are times in our lives when everything ends and we begin again with nothing. It is not that the past is wholly lost, but it will seem that way. It is not that the future is devoid of hope—the future will have no apparent meaning.

Transition is always ritualized, by which I mean that what is happening deep within our spirit is always expressed in outer symbolical behavior. The behavior does not have to be elaborate, nor does it have to be something that we never did before. What happens is that our actions take on a whole new meaning. We are suddenly confronted with the unexpected and the unknown, the reality that has become something of a mystery, and our response to it will either renew us or be destructive.

The ritual of transition can never be rushed; growth is a slow process. At first there may be matters of a business nature which need attention, the proper goodbyes (refusing to be petty) to be said when indicated. We go from there to working patiently through anxieties and frustrations. We gentle our feelings, quieting the dogs of resentment which keep barking in our memories. We find new things to do, ask questions, accept advice and pray. In the end we grow into freedom and come to decisions. It takes time, and the understanding of what is happening to us comes through the medium of the ritual itself.

For example, a widow might look at the photographs of her deceased husband, and ask some very positive questions: "What did you mean to me? What is this all about? How shall I cope without you? What do I do now?" The questions themselves will lead her into a spiritual journey, and ultimately to the resolution of her transition. We all ritualize, because we all go back to examine the meaning of the

5

profound experiences of life, the happy as well as the painful. It may be no more than looking at old photographs, or going back to the place of one's birth, or driving out to see the place where one worked. I have known men who returned to France to see again the places where they fought in World War II. And criminals, they say, return to the scene of the crime. It is all ritual. And its purpose is to prevent the past getting bottled up inside us as a destructive force.

There is a destructive ritual. It happens when a person refuses to accept the reality of his transition. We are aware of the stereotype of the unemployed who sits before the television drinking beer all day. It is a ritualization of defeat, a protection against the pain that the world inflicted, a pain that might have brought about growth. There is the familiar story of the widow who leaves her husband's room exactly as it was the day he died. It is also a refusal to embark on a journey of discovery and of human growth. It is not outside the realm of possibility for even suicide, the final ritualistic act of defeat, to take place when the spiritual journey of transition is refused.

My own inner journeying began when, after nine years as a chaplain to a community of Benedictine Sisters, it was felt that a change was necessary. We chaplains are a somewhat seedy lot. We are of no importance whatever in the institutional aspect of the Church. We are vulnerable, too, being something of a commodity on the market, advertised for in the religious press, hired, controlled and fired by the heads of institutions. And the Christian corporate structure does not always do the firing with finesse. For all the value of our ministry, our role in the structure is minor, walking two steps behind the monarch while citizens disguised as sparrows twitter in our belfries. Most of us are periodically reminded that we would not have been hired at all were it not that the eucharistic liturgy has to be celebrated. If we happen to survive at all, it is by reaching a concerned, if modest level of serene involvement. It is imperative that we be not too insightful, articulate or creative, lest in being so we become a threat to the crown.

As for myself, I was uppity. Indeed, looking back on it now, I was arrogant. I had to go. Yet, I felt crushed inside. Cushioning the disaster, however, was the feeling that, with some wry justice, the rabid feminism with which I had defended the flock had been dealt an enlightening blow. Very conservatively, I quit the active ministry, and returned to my abbey.

I began the ritual by disposing of everything. On leaving the priory in Idaho, I gave a tape recorder to one, records to another, books to several. Whatever could be hauled away was cheerfully hauled off by somebody, and the rest—old photographs, clothing, notebooks—got placed in two-ply Hefty bags and deposited in the local garbage collection bin. Clean sweep!

My friends asked that they be allowed to store some things for me, on the grounds that I would never fit back into the abbey. Despite my own doubts about fitting back in, I felt that if I were to return at all I should do so absolutely, hence the clean sweep. I had more good faith than good sense. For one thing, I had just completed a small manuscript on the subject of chaos, a work in praise of human freedom, of standing unfettered by routine so that one might receive the spark of creativity and growth when it fell. It took a dim view of unchanging order, feeling that out of such routine can come only "more of the same." My friends assured me that it was an expression of myself, and that there was no way I could go back again to the ordered life of the abbey. I did not listen to them. But, then, I do not always listen to my own heart which tells me that order and discipline are values which I might do well to cultivate. However, I had to return, if for no other reason than to settle my relationship to these monks and to this life.

Another factor militating against my fitting in was the meaningfulness I found in active ministry, the conviction that we receive from God what we pass on to others, gifts that are received in the very act of ministering. Desires for an active ministry are very suspect in a cloistered community.

There was some enlightment, also. I had come to see that people of a contemplative bent amongst the laity, and in the active ministries, were quite as authentic and profound as those in the enclosure. One does not have to be in a cloister to be a contemplative. The enclosure, they tell me, simplifies life, yet it is not life but we ourselves who need simplifying, if we are to outgrow our devotion to arbitrary structures. The religious life is not so much a consecration to God, which might well make one quite smug, as the placing of oneself totally at the disposal of God. Being at God's disposal is always an open-ended and risky way of life.

I have many friends. In that I am fortunate, and it humbles me. I single out four from the many, because they are very special to me.

7

We go back many years. I miss them now. Two of them drove me down from the priory in Idaho to my abbey here in Utah. The father of one of them had recently died, so we talked mostly of his death and of her time of mourning. She needed to talk it out. But I was sad at the thought of parting from them and unable to be fully present to her. She also was in transition, and her talking, like their driving me down, was part of the ritual. We drove past little towns called Eden, Bliss and Paradise Valley. The irony of it struck me, there being little that was blissful in leaving my work, my friends and the places I had come to love. Beyond Rupert we turned right and headed down toward Ogden. I had a chill in my blood as we crossed the state line into Utah. Part of it was closing the door on Idaho, part of it was facing the oppressive atmosphere of neo-gnosticism one meets everywhere in Utah, though the kindness of the people is without question.

We had lunch in Ogden. I gave my friends the few dollars and loose change I had, and handed over the keys of the car. It was a sort of symbolical gesture, an ending. The old clunker had more than a quarter million miles on it and it had almost become part of me. In fact, the novices and I had celebrated its two hundred thousand mark with a party. We got in the car and drove out to the abbey.

There was snow on the ground and on the abbey buildings when we got there. The abbey is built of large Quonset huts, four sections welded together to form a quadrangle. It is poor, as monastic buildings should be, yet the curved roofs blend in well with the surrounding hills. Inside, it is quite a pleasant place. I dropped off my bag, and we sat and had a cup of coffee. We made the kind of meaningless small talk people make when they care for each other and are about to part, perhaps not to meet again. One of the two had tears on her face. Afterward we drove down the road a half-mile where we made our goodbyes. There was a depth of sadness snatching at my heart as we parted. Then I stood in the road and watched the car drive off and get smaller in the distance until it disappeared from view. I realized how thoroughly I was cut off, in this monastic enclosure, from the people and places I had come to love. I turned and walked back to the abbey with no feeling at all for it.

Days have passed. The silence is cosmic. I have a small room over which the Quonset roof curves. I am back in routine and coping poorly with it. No spark has fallen from heaven, but the roof has fallen in and chaos lies like rubble round my feet. I am not adjusting well. I have no notion where this transition is leading, perhaps nowhere. My nights are a balancing act on a small cot. It is difficult to get to sleep when we retire at 8 P.M., and when I sleep I dream of being at war, of being bombed and shot, being full of fear.

The abbot is kind and understanding, and the monks with the exception of a few have been warm in their welcome. I am quite well aware that no manner of life, no group of individuals, is absolutely perfect, not here, not anywhere. I accept that. I am not looking for utopia. But my mind is abstracted. I come to myself at times realizing that I have been praying to my friends and not to God. If doing unto others is doing to God, perhaps praying to my friends, in the sense of needing others, is an expression of needing God.

The sun is shining on the snow. The valley is a place of brittle beauty. My lungs hurt from the icy air and my breath floats away in fog as I walk across the fields to the feed-lot at the foot of the hills. It is a few days before Christmas. Nick and Michael were at the feed-lot, sitting on upturned crates under a lean-to, taking a break from work. There was straw, which did not look all that clean, strewn around. Michael rose from the crate and sat on the straw, insisting that I should take his place. It is this kind of small but genuine act of courtesy, or love—whatever one might call it—that makes me believe in these men and in the possibilities of this life. Nick is the only man I have ever found who could give me insightful spiritual direction. In going to the heart and truth of a situation, bypassing all pseudo problems, he shows the rare gift of what, in monastic language, is called discretion. I am fortunate to be close to him. Michael is one of the gentle people of the earth who will receive heaven as a gift.

It was good sitting out there, feeling the warmth of the sun and watching it sparkle on the snow. Only a half-dozen miles across from us, Mount Ogden stood four thousand feet over the little valley, and a few miles north the point of Ben Lomond was clean and white against the blue sky. It had lifting power for my heart. I could hear mice rustling under the straw; they felt friendly. It was good to be close to the earth.

I have been assigned to the egg department for my daily work detail. It is a strange contrast from giving workshops, prayer days and the ministry I had to a religious community. The department is

9

housed in a large metal building a couple of hundred yards down from the abbey. The novices and I work there in a section next to where seven-and-a-half thousand chickens are caged. There are two, sometimes three chickens in each cage and the arrangement is reasonably humane. They are automatically fed all they can eat, and are more free of disease than those which run loose. Were they able to reflect on their encagement as I am on mine, however, it would be quite another matter. There is, of course, the problem with cannibalism. As among nations, so among chickens. Space, privilege and status are established in cosmic cage through the pecking process. Chickens are debeaked (arms limitation) by removing a small bit of the tip of the beak, to prevent their drawing blood. But peck they will, even to death, and there is no malice. It just feels good.

One monk supervises the egg washing, one candles them—removing those with cracks and blood spots—and one packs them in Jumbo, Extra-Large, Large, Medium and Peewee sizes. I do the packing at the moment, three dozen a minute, aided by a suction affair which picks them up. In automated work, one must take the speed of the machine which has no respect whatever for one's psychological speed. The work is sufficiently interesting—though never creative—to keep us from becoming catatonic, and sufficiently boring to allow for thought or prayer. The novices are very pleasant people and do not lose their cool. One of them, a huge Texan who played football for Purdue, hollers, "Baw-w-w-y, will you git this thang outa heyah!" Everybody smiles. Afterward we clean up and go to church.

I have had a small surprise, a half dozen copies in the mail of *The Experience of Praying*. It has been reprinted in paperback. I can pass them around among a few people here who would like to read it. There was a note from Paulist Press' Managing Editor, Don Brophy. He is reading *Chaos* and likes it. He is concerned about my re-entry. In the world of business, I find him unique, very personal and very encouraging.

I pray a bit before I retire to fight my wars in my dreams. I tell God that since I am a celibate monk, my religious commitment, community, God himself must come before my ministry and my friends. I must let go of the past. I tell him that I cannot find it in me to let go. I ask him what it is that I am doing here, what the meaning of my life is—at one time I thought I knew. I realize, for a moment of intensity, a presence of God, that he emptied himself and that he is now emptying me. I know in my heart that there will be no false pity in him, and I do not like the thought. I know that he is calling me to some inner change.

I pray for the thousands who are in transition, who have to change, and who know perfectly well that they cannot return to the past. I can see that it is a death and resurrection affair. The deepest option for life will be in the transition. We are challenged. The future will be a rising to a greater human wholeness or it will be nothing at all.

I end with a prayer for my friends.

2. The Role of Friends

Wherever there are authentic friendships, friendships which are final and valid forever because they emerge from, and are grounded in, people's ultimate purpose in existing, there God, Christ and Christian living are made real.

Friends keep us honest. We need them. In a time of transition, they are an invaluable support. They help shape our entire spiritual journey. I think of all the people in the world who have never had a friend, who have never felt loved, or supported, or encouraged to grow. I feel sad for them. I think also of the many who have been offered friendship and have not recognized it, or have been too busy to cultivate it. Those of us who have friends are many times blest.

I feel close to people who have lost loved ones, and I have some sense of what the transition must be for them. My own friends are not entirely lost, yet something has ended and I feel it. Although sentiment is a valid part of our humanness, I do not propose to be sentimental. But I certainly am not indifferent. I can share best about the important role of friendship only by telling what my friends meant to me.

My mind slips back on the paths of memory and I am filled with thoughts of the many things we shared—little things such as laughing together over food in a restaurant, skipping stones on the water, pushing driftwood logs into the river, sharing jokes, talking; and bigger things: comforting them in family bereavements, supporting them when they were harassed in their ministry, struggling with them for insights into the ways of God, doing liturgies, workshops and prayer-days with them. Here, in my enclosed life, I find it difficult to admit, because I do not want to admit, that the path of life has many branches, that people separate and life moves on. Part of my transition is to experience this separation, and to know that it is the lot of people everywhere. My head tells me that it will be all right; my heart disagrees. It is just that head and heart are male and female, and jealous of their independence. My heart can feel loss while my head talks logic, and, then again, my heart can be like ice while my head begs for compassion. At this point in my transition, I have not yet begun to come to grips with reality. It is still a time of looking back and of feelings. But I know, also, that feelings cannot be denied.

To live the life of a full human person has relatively little to do with being healthy, wealthy, successful and wise. To be human is to be in good relationships with others. It is in that respect that my friends were, and I trust will continue to be, crucial to my life.

The first, of four I single out, was the only authentic, natural-born contemplative I have ever known. She had the harmony of a soul-friend. Without any forethought whatever, she would mention a book that I should read, and it would turn out to be the one book I most needed. She would mention music, and I would find it fitting perfectly into my prayer life. She directed me to Mahler, to Beethoven's *Violin Concerto*, Samuel Barber's *Adagio for Strings*, medieval English music, even to Carl Orff's *Carmina Burana* (which didn't help my prayer) and to much more. She would mention something offhand, and it would become incarnated in something creative in my life. It was clear to me that God was working through her in my regard. We could share ideas in very few words. We talked of the mystery of God in ways that made no logic, but were full of meaning. She hardly knew she had that way. She does not belong in the world of organized enterprises. The organizers are puzzled by her. In a pragmatic world she endures much misunderstanding. Yet, her way is the music of life.

My second friend would seem to be the direct opposite, but she is as truly a friend. She is precise, organized, knows her business. She is capable and independent. She pushed and pressured, argued and supported me. Should I happen to mention a need, she would depart and later return with five possible avenues of solution, all of them worked out with names, addresses, and phone numbers. When I doubted myself, she would be uncompromising, pooh-poohing my weakness as unworthy. I owe a great deal to her.

The third friend should be called my theologian. She knew her

13

theology, and it had the grace of coming from her heart as well as from her head. She had a direct, even insistent, way of getting to the truth. She allowed nobody to get away with ideas that were soft or bent. But she was full of caring, so that at times it was difficult to know where the caring ended and the hard-nosed theologian took over. She was not at all, in regard to me or to others, about to look upon men as better informed by virtue of the fact that they were men, or were ordained. It has cost her much, but her friendship taught me something about integrity.

The fourth taught me one unique aspect of friendship—its impact on community. If it is sincere, it builds; if it is phony it destroys. She challenged my sincerity. She showed me that true friendship has to be totally unselfish, that if it is not it undermines togetherness. She taught me that any attitude of exclusiveness, or manipulation would be a violation of community, a destructive force. She could teach me that because she was without any such faults herself. I had not thought in such terms, feeling that friendship was a private concern and not the business of others. She showed me how phony that could be. Her concept of friendship was positive and so laughingly alive that in the end she became a sort of sacrament, a visible sign of God's love for me. That overflowed into my understanding of the depths of the friendships of others. She is responsible for my writing, although, needless to say, my organizational friend nagged me all the way to the publisher. There are other friends, male and female, men like Nick, and a few married couples, who influence my life.

I took these four for granted, possibly because they were so alive, mature, intelligent, and so absolutely committed to their ministry in the Church. It did not occur to me that I should one day be separated from them. I hardly knew how they had shaped and supported me. I know now that we priests have very much to learn and gain from both sisters and laity, and for my own part I think it is about time to acknowledge it. How unfree many of us are in this respect.

I had a letter from the East Coast, from a young woman I knew years ago. She is now divorced, in her mid-thirties, delightful, devout, an artist, who teaches religion to a group of high school youths. The letter was all about her job. I was going through it in a detached sort of way when all of a sudden she woke me up. She had been saying how outgoing, attractive and receptive the seventeen year old boys were, how good it was to teach them, and then quite casually remarked how she gets "sexually aroused teaching them the parables in Matthew." I responded with what P.G. Wodehouse calls "the sharp intake of breath and the upraised eyebrow." That small bit of information seemed to have little place in a Trappist setting, and may seem to have slight purpose in my writing here, but, in fact, it was important within my experience of transition. It was not the erotic element that got my attention—well, yes, that was O.K. too, but it was not my main interest. I was surprised by the honest, human, normalcy of someone who could write about such a matter.

But it was more than that: after weeks of exclusively male society where masculine dullness has reached alarming proportions, I had arrived at a point where the female half of the species was receding into a myth from the past. It is difficult to realize within this enclosure that there really is another half to the human family. One rarely, or never, encounters it. It is more difficult still to accept the fact that women are complementary, not just the enemy. There is a monastic opinion of many centuries' standing that monks are better off not knowing women. ("Beware bishops and women," as the Desert Fathers would have it.) It seems to me that one would have to be very cynical indeed to accept that. My correspondent's remark was just enough of a mild shock to get me laughing about life.

In an all-male community, the reality of women has no place. People feel that it is quite possible to get along very well without them. But it is a strange thing: I feel as if half of me were missing. In fact, I know it, and I see signs of that absence in some of the people around me. Personality is, after all, tied up with relationships. The friends I knew challenged one's thinking and feelings, and the expressions of both.

The demand that one not think and act as if men were the only species on earth is vital to men's growth. And the occasional TV presentation of women as being something less than mature should alert them to accept a like challenge from men. The male/female dualism we have fostered, and which amongst celibates we have decreed, is wholly without justification in Christianity. I sometimes wonder about some of the directives issuing from the Vatican: are they an expression of an isolated enclave of all-male bachelors who are not even aware of how deprived they are? Without the challenge of those who complement us, we lose our capacity to feel. In a time of transition, that is a loss we cannot afford. Those friendships civilize us.

Christmas eve arrived. I stopped in to speak to the abbot. He was very gracious, assuring me that my friends may visit. I told him that I could not make much sense of this place, that I am finding it difficult to accept it, that my return was the result of circumstances, that had my chaplaincy been extended I would not have returned. I mentioned that my head was not getting me anywhere, that reason and logic are lost on me.

We discussed *The Experience of Praying* and some of the passages which seemed to create an unfavorable image of the monks—it had created some controversy in the abbey and in the Order. He told me that the abbot general felt it was reasonably all right. Time, I feel, will heal many things within and about me. In view of Don Brophy's liking *Chaos*, and the possibility of its acceptance for publication, I decided to ask him if he would have a monk, whose name I mentioned, read the manuscript—after the experience of my first book, the second has to be censored. He agreed to that, and said that it was only a formality.

Christmas eve was not so felicitous in the egg department. My back and leg muscles protested sharply as I bent over the machine. The burly novice in charge of washing was moody and not paying attention, with the result that too many soiled eggs were coming through. We had to shut down the operation time and again to get them sandpapered clean. As a safety valve, I recalled a time in the past when I picked up a case of thirty dozen eggs on flats, only to have the bottom fall out of the case. It was one of those magnificent moments. They had to be shoveled up. There is a moment in everybody's life when one deserves the thrill of smashing three hundred and sixty eggs in one great filthy splash! Just thinking about it had power to delight my heart. But we got through the work and saved our sense of balance. I thought of Christmas and of my friends. Perhaps all of us did—I see signs of it in the novice. I have the hope that Christmas will be helpful, but I have no enthusiasm for it.

Tomorrow, I shall go for a walk in the hills with Nick.

The wintry sun drops behind Mount Ogden, and night comes quickly. I sit in my dark room in prayer:

I have a clear mental image of standing with my friends beneath the crucifixion of our togetherness. I say, "Togetherness, if you are God, come down from the cross." I think, "What if togetherness could not die on the cross, would there be anyone to put it out of its misery?"

I fight off the sentimentality and ask God, "Why transition? Is it blind fate? Is it freedom's chaos? Is the cause within myself in some personality flaw? What is the flaw? What did I do wrongly? Is the cause outside myself in somebody's ambition, or jealousy, or overbearing attitude? I feel guilty, Lord."

3. Guilt at Christmastime

Only those who search, and wait, and hunger can one day celebrate.
But there is no celebration until the transition is resolved and all the
anxiety is reduced to absurdity.

In a time of transition, we do battle with all that is negative. We
fight off defeat. In fact, we suffer from a big dose of guilt. This
happens even though there is no specific thing about which to feel
guilty. It would hardly seem to be the apt subject for reflection on
Christmas day. But, then, Christmas has never been a very good day
for bachelors, to say nothing of people in transition. It is probably
the happiest and saddest day of the year for many people.

This form of vague but very real sense of guilt surfaces for the
very simple reason that our deepest instinct suggests that our present
reality should not be what it is. So we slight ourselves. We think that
God is punishing us, that he has condemned us for some real or
imaginary failure. The bad theology we were taught about God in
our youth comes to the forefront of our thinking. We see ourselves as
the dead branches that had to be lopped off and thrown on the fire.
Even when our head tells us that we are talking nonsense, our heart is
not so sure.

This sense of guilt is an important element in our ongoing
spiritual journey. The very first thing we should be clear about is that
this is not a personal guilt. It is not arising from something we did, or
left undone. One can hear this sense of guilt in the extravagant
statements of people in transition: "If only I had done such and such,
the accident would not have happened . . . he would not have left me
. . . she would still be alive . . . I would not have been dismissed," and
so on." But all of that is pure hindsight, sheer illusion. What is really

happening is that we are beginning to sense the deep unconscious guilt that is the heritage of centuries of conflict with God, the disharmony of an enclosed world with the God who is calling it forth. It surfaces in people when they are not at one with themselves or when they fail to understand what is happening to them.

This is not some neurotic anxiety. It is deeper and more healthy than that. What is happening is that transition is beginning to break us out of our narrow self-enclosed world and opening us up to humanity at large. We never before needed humanity at large. Now we sense the universality of the problem we all have with God—humanity rebellious, out of step with God's plan for it, guilty, but also repentant, loved and saved.

This sense of guilt is actually a call to become more free, to discover the truth of what the world is all about and to develop compassion. It is a call to the acceptance of ourselves, clay feet and all, so that we might make the gift of ourselves to others. When that acceptance comes, we shall experience the salvation of the world as something which takes place within each one of us. It is true that this guilt creates tensions, but their purpose is to lead us to a higher truth, the truth that will set us free. We may not even know that such a truth exists. If we do, we long for it, and for a time we do not seem to have it. We need some kind of breakthrough. Once we get over our irrational guilt, this truth will enable us to act creatively, to take responsibility again for our lives in decision making, to be more fully human. It will enable us to take ourselves in hand and commit ourselves to life in a way that has a definitiveness about it.

The truth that will emerge has something to do with what reality is, our reality within the reality of God, life, world and purpose. What can we discover about our existence that we have not thus far found out? Before God, who or what shall we now be? The purpose of the guilt was not to make us think ill of ourselves, but to push us along into those basic questions. It was a bad experience which got us into transition. What we have to do now is to sit in silence and digest this experience in our minds until the truth comes. It should be clear enough that acting stubbornly and conservatively, licking our wounds and entertaining thoughts of bitterness or self-destruction can only hold up our journey. We do not have to deny the hurt. We have to be expanded within our spirit from it. The challenge of our transition is that we fashion our time into a positive future.

19

It rained all of Christmas day. The burly novice left us without saying goodbye. He wrote a note and took off in his pickup. He was free to leave. I hope that he will be all right, but I do not envy him. Freedom does not consist in the ability to take off. It is something inside oneself, finding oneself within the freedom of Christ's response to the Father, being able to be at the Father's disposal. At the liturgy, the abbot called us all to vulnerability, to dropping our protective shields, so that a deeper love might be possible. Then we ate our Christmas dinner in silence. I wondered what incarnation was all about. If it was the ultimate consecration of all that was most fully human, what were we doing eating in silence? I don't know. Perhaps I am missing something. And I do not want to be fed some nonsense about the depths of people's contemplation. It isn't that.

Nick and I went for a walk into the hills, despite the rain. We went up past where my hermitage of years ago had been. There were a few concrete blocks still scattered around, but the broken-down mobile home that had been my dwelling had been sold for a hundred dollars.

There was sadness on the hills. Low grey clouds clung to them, and rain fell most of the time. We went up the draw through trees which were stripped of leaves, sloshing along in mud and water, our heads down because of the rain. We talked a lot, but there was no breakthrough in my thinking. I had thought that on Christmas day God would do or say something, or give me some sort of sign. I tried to explain to Nick something of what transition is, the feeling of being uprooted, of being in an alien culture, one's feelings in disharmony with reason, the disrupted relationships, the absence of something meaningful to do. He did not reply, as he might very well have done, that what I was experiencing was no big deal. Instead, he told me how much he himself felt caught up into what was going on inside me. That, I think, was God's gift to me. What more could one ask of a friend?

We circled around and came down across the hills to the abbey. Nick is a strong man, his mind as mild as summer. He is well adjusted to this place, and not for any illusory reasons. Life is a gift he gives away. He does not stop to think of any form of gain, of being this or that, or anything else which in his eyes would only be a false image. He is genuine.

I showered and went to church where we sang Vespers. The

20

hours in church are quiet, peaceful times. Prayer is normally a time of great relaxation for me, not as a technique, of course, but as a by-product. But during transition we all find it difficult to be quiet within our minds. As for myself, the moment I sit in silent prayer my mind swings wildly from God to guilt, to life, to death, to trust and back to God again. Relaxing, however, has to be a part of transition's ritual. We cannot stay wound up. I listen to a composite tape I put together some time ago. On it are Samuel Barber's *Adagio for Strings*, the sound of waves breaking on the sand at Carmel-by-the-Sea, and some readings from the poetry of Robinson Jeffers about the California coast. It takes me completely out of myself and refreshes my mind.

The monks vanished into their rooms and Christmas day faded away into the silence of this dimly lit abbey. I sat down again on a cushion with my back to the wall and tried to pray before retiring.

I stare into the darkness. I acknowledge the outer calm and security of my life, the logic of it all. I acknowledge also the flea of discontent that exists in my brain. I quiet myself before God and ask for mercy.

I seem to move out into space and be lost there. It is a strange experience. There is nothing at all on which I can build something, a thought, an understanding, a purpose. I have no feeling; it is as if I have died but cannot find my way to heaven. I grasp at one reality, that of a friend as being the sacrament of God's love for me. It is an anchor hold, the only thing I can see or touch between God's absence and my being here. If I did not have friends, I feel that I would disappear altogether. I am grateful for their love, less than a child for their caring.

I pray that people everywhere will be happy, celebrating around Christmas trees.

4. Reality or Unreality

When reality is stressful, we have clever ways of coping. One way or another, we are determined to survive.

I have been thinking a great deal about reality/unreality. I have the feeling that it is an extremely important issue in our transitional journey. The willingness to accept reality is central. But what is reality? Even Einstein had trouble with that question. We have a partial grasp on things.

My reflections were brought on by a strange sense of communion I seemed to have with another person's spirit. I had been sitting here at my desk making an attempt to read in a dull, sleepy sort of way, my mind abstracted. Suddenly, I felt as if one of my friends were here beside me. It was a good experience and I felt better afterward. Later, I felt that if I concentrated, I could at any time be in touch with her spirit, and cease to feel entirely alone. It was a bit vague and nebulous, but I wonder if I'm cracking up.

The silence in the abbey (not absolute, but nearly so), the lack of communication—conversations, travel, TV, radio—the difficulty I am having with prayer and reading, the sense of being out in space, all seem to be edging me toward some form of mild breakdown. What would make for the breakdown would be the substitution of the unreal for the real. This place is certainly real. So is my presence here, for all that I question the purpose of it. But this concentrated ordered life, the unchanging daily schedule, and the needlessness of so many of its elements are making it easy for me to convince myself of its entire unreality. In this frame of mind, I go looking for what is real. I say to myself that the past and the people I knew in it are my reality.

Because of my present meaninglessness I long for those people's presence. I know in my head that they cannot be present, but my feelings do not know that.

The breakdown would be simple: if I concentrate on my feelings, and if I use the powers of my imagination, I know now that I could go through a sort of mental reorientation. I have experienced a few flashes of it, like a wave breaking over my nervous system. In this reorientation, being in the past would become my reality, and being here would recede into fantasy. I had always thought that a mental or emotional breakdown was something violent, or incoherent, or illogical. In fact, it is a magnificently clever manner of survival when one refuses the challenge to accept the reality at hand. It is a calm choice, innocently made, perhaps even without reflection, of substituting a fantasy from the past for one's present reality. I have enough self-reflection not to do that—enough sense too—but I can see where I could have headed in the wrong direction. I am certain now of one thing: I am not going to crack up. What will prevent its happening is this curiosity I have, the need to analyze and reflect on every experience so as to learn something from it.

For the past few weeks, my friends have been a support, their letters and friendship keeping me alive in a reality which seemed so sterile. I longed for the past to the degree that I could become mentally disoriented, were it not for my curiosity. I could not opt out of reality without watching myself do it, and that, in itself, was a function of reason sufficient to keep me sane.

⌈ Now that I realize the mental and emotional tricks I have been playing, I am aware of the need to make a choice: to live in the warm comfort of an illusion, or to let the past be past and accept for now the reality of my being here.⌋I have chosen the second and feel a bit sad in so doing. But I feel that I have won a victory of sorts, and have written to a friend and asked her to break out a bottle of Pepsi to celebrate it. I forego the presence of my friends, but not themselves. And I feel that I have learned something about reality. Though the real here is not more purposeful for me, nor the unreal less alluring— the fantasies, illusions, wishful thinking—things are now in better place.

⌊ What I have to say to people in transition is this: be honest; the past was never as perfect as we are now inclined to think it was. And stick with the present reality, even if it hurts. To have failed, to have

23

lost somebody or something, or to have been hurt is not the end of everything. Nothing succeeds like letting go of hurt. In my own case, separation is real, and so is the friendship; the commitment to live a full life in ministry to others is real, and so is the pain in sitting around doing nothing; the surrender to God in vows is real, and so is the price. But wishful thinking, vain expectations and the thoughts that come out of feelings alone are mostly unreal. The real in life is gain and loss, laughter and hurt, love and vulnerability.

Of course, that is easy to say and not always easy to do. I have no desire to indulge in farmyard smells, to stuff myself into the soiled clothing on going out to work, to live in deadly routine, to be incarcerated. No doubt about it, as monks go I have clay feet. A "good monk," I am told, has no desires. But this bit of simple wisdom exasperates me to an outburst: "Who the hell wants to be labeled 'Good'?" I just want to be myself, flaws and all, to reach out, to be able to share myself with others. I am caught in a trap, searching for insight and understanding. The struggle with reality will continue for quite some time. But at least I am saying to myself that it's time I got on with the business of living.

In a time of transition, we are caught in a tension between two realities: the desire our human spirit has for something absolute and stable, and the present experience of limitations. Whether we are aware of it or not, the human spirit has an instinct which refuses to recognize limitations, to be satisfied with them. It is a function of this spiritual journey of ours to be alerted to this. For too long we have been satisfied with the distractions at hand. But the distractions and the limitations now oppress us. We long for limitless fulfillment. Without this tension between limits and the hunger for something absolute, there would be no growth. Now we can confront reality, defy the irrational and destructive elements in our lives and in our spirit transcend them, even if, in the end, they are never fully overcome. Life is passionate, and it is given to us to be celebrated passionately. The goal in life is not the quieting of powerful passions—a Greek idea—but the proper use of them—a biblical idea.

If we enter fully into our experience of living, something we are challenged to do at this time, we inevitably improve the quality of life. If we claim that we are in possession of our lives, that we are human at all, then our integrity demands that we probe life's meaning. Not only should we question ourselves and our prior naive notions, we should question and examine the assumptions of others about life. We should challenge their ways of thinking and behavior, not to deny but to improve life and explore it. There are all kinds of assumptions about the good life, about success and failure, health and handicaps, gain and loss, pain and death that have to be called into question. This may very well lead to a clash with elements which deny growth, or with those who see their role as enforcing conformity. We should not fear them. Life has to be lived with the totality of our spirit, even when in doing so we are misunderstood by others, or wounded by the paradoxes of a broken world.

The monastic *quies*, resting contemplatively in God, with which I struggle here, is neither the meek collapse of a beaten person who thinks he has left the world, nor an unconcern for others. It is a harmony and union between an absolutely uncontrollable God, but a God who cares, and a searching, growing, passionate human person. That harmony is possible without the destruction of anything in our humanness, even when by age, or loss, or illness the outer circumstances of reality have changed or disintegrated. It may not be possible without pain, but pain is not necessarily destructive. Its purpose is to alert us to reality.

To turn away from stressful reality, I seek for ways to relax. And I have found a way which I enjoy, dipping into the volumes of the *Acts of the General Chapters* of our Order. They are written in Latin, and nobody bothers to read them. Now, that might not seem to be very entertaining, but they are quite enjoyable, and without intending to do so they give a very realistic picture of monks and the Church in earlier centuries. For example: the abbots of the Order, assembled in Chapter in the year of Our Lord, 1413, ". . . deplore the fact that abbesses and some nuns are wearing such tight clothing that their breasts and buttocks protrude immodestly in a manner that offends the laity." The abbots, naturally, were against it. That was five hundred and sixty-nine years ago. With my warped sense of humor at the incongruous solemnity of the corporate structure, I think that is very funny. And I walk out of the library with a smile on my face, holding the condition of things in a nice proportion within my mind. One must admit that the abbots had imagination.

The realm of the writer or the artist is imagination—the ability to put images on experiences—which is why so many of them cracked up, some ending their own lives. They were aware that the unreal, the fantasy, had oftentimes more truth, more interest and entertainment, more insight than the dull facts of the real world. But to keep one's mental health intact, one has to live in the real, if dull, world. Unlike Van Gogh, I have no intention at this point of cutting off my ear and sending it to the Pope. However, I must admit that I would love to sit down with my friends in a restaurant, as we used to, and thrash out all this mystery of reality/unreality, laughing together with delight in our hearts.

It is evening and early winter darkness. The abbey sits in the middle of a snow-covered valley, frozen to silence under a clear sky. The field reflects a dark blue light. The house is still, not a whisper of sound. I sit in my dark room, praying to Absolute Silence. I beg for a word, any word, but God is mute. I am on a spaceship, drifting through the dark blue light. I pray from some far distant corner of space. I have lost touch with the earth. The crew does its daily chores, not questioning why they are drifting. Surely, Lord, they have great faith, while here I am in exodus hankering for the fleshpots of Egypt. But there is no Moses and no Sinai on the horizon.

My God, I am real. I convince myself of that. And there are people caring and loving; there are highways and cars, cities and friendly people somewhere.

God, is not friendship the serious business of life? Is it not the business of the married as much as it is of the rest of us? Does not friendship humanize and spiritualize the world? I am concerned—a celibate without a friend is a man without God. I feel humbled by the love my friends have for me. I ask you, Father-God, to bless them and people everywhere.

For all those in transition I pray: "The Lord will keep you from evil; he will keep your life. The Lord will keep your going out and your coming in from this time and for evermore" (Psalm 121).

5. The Basic Questions

If this were a novel, the plot might thicken and satisfy you, like a good soup on a winter's day. But it's not a novel. I'm serving up life, and life in transition is a casserole of leftovers. We have questions, mainly: "What's in it?"

Transition has this good purpose: it compels us to ask fundamental questions. Why are we here? Does life have any meaning? What do we expect to get out of it? Where are we going? Bereaved, fired from a job, critically injured, divorced, we ask the crucial question, the most religious question of all: "What purpose does our existence have?" It is a religious question because it examines life in the light of ultimate values. The relative values have failed us and now we are up against the crucial question.

We also question God. We question our relationship, if any, to him. Do we have a spiritual life? Are we on a spiritual journey? What can we learn from the experience?

To fail to question the transition in the context of what meaning it has for our life as a whole is to wind up inevitably in tragedy. We either become bitter, or slump in defeat, or go on repeating the original mistakes leading to further disappointments. It is easy to turn away from the questions; there is a temptation to avoid the challenge of life by turning to something distracting or entertaining —some task at hand, endless talk, soap operas. Or it is possible to say that the questions have no answers, and turn away in depression or despair, maintaining that life is meaningless. Much of life is indeed absurd, at least if we do not have a very deep faith dimension, and it would be false to deny the depths of its loneliness. The concerned

27

person will, however, ask questions. No transition is so absolutely a tragedy that it should lead to despair. It should, in the end, be the saving of the whole purpose of our life.

Our world has changed with sudden pain, and we ask: "Why?" One insight that begins to emerge, a vague discovery of ours, is that up until now our attention had been too closely concentrated on something finite—status, job, relationship, self-image, possessions or whatever—and now we are being called out to experience the entire purpose of life, the broader picture. There was too much emptiness there all along, and it took the sudden shock of transition to expose it. Now that our fixation on the finite has been removed we have been cast back on ourselves. But the honest question "Why?" puts us in touch with the whole of our existence. It returns us to our source, to the ground of our existence. The finite failed us, and now our very helplessness, our anxiety, and our compulsive sense of obligation become the very mediums of a spiritual journey toward the ultimate meaning of life.

It is true that we are floundering about in this mystery of our existence, but we cannot be expected to know where the journey is leading until the journey ends. In the past we got trapped in one small part of who we are and forgot our existence as a whole. Letting go of the small part of who we were, and forcibly, as it were, being made to consider the entire picture, is very painful. This is a disguised, but very real blessing. We might avoid it by hardening our hearts, but then we would pay a much larger price.

Besides questioning the transition, we also question our own personal reality with its varied elements—its fears and hopes, its needs and stress. In so questioning, we establish the fact that we are greater than the sum of our many elements. We do this by standing outside ourselves and calling ourselves into question. This opens us up to all kinds of creative possibilities. When we pause to reflect on it, we find that who we are is always greater than all that can be called into question, greater than the outer circumstances which brought us into transition, greater than the disappointments, failures, accomplishments or rejections. On this spiritual journey we are called to be someone, rather than to achieve something. The questions emerge from the mystery, God himself, who is calling us to become who we are supposed to be. The Spirit within us questions, thereby surpassing, all the finite things which bother us.

28

But we also question God himself, and that is proper. We may and we should question God for the simple reason that we are persons, and not objects. We question God so as to deepen our awareness of what the deity is all about, and what place he has in our lives. We question God by asking why he permits suffering, why he is so silent, whether he cares or not, whether he can help us. The answers will come in a very slow paradoxical manner. His ways and thoughts and language are not ours, and it takes a while to learn them. But to blame God or get angry with him, as if he were some kind of objectivized functionary, makes no kind of theological sense whatever. The challenge we face is to stop thinking of God with our continued childhood assumptions, and to grow. It is a challenge to whatever spirituality we have.

We question the future as the place where we might meet God. We are forced to ask whether or not we mean anything to him. Because if we mean nothing to him we are worthless, and we are not free. The silence of God to our questioning may be a crushing experience. If we mean nothing, why does he permit us to go on living? And if we do mean something to him—and he died to convince us that we do—then we must discover in the silence and darkness of our faith a new self-worth of which we are as yet unaware. Getting there is the pattern of this journey.

The reality, of course, is that we are loved absolutely. This love, in turn, creates a sort of absolute worth within ourselves, not some relative worth which in the past arose from our accomplishments. Our true worth will call us out from our absorption in the finite to celebrate life absolutely, and together with all life in the universe. We are being called to a personal maturity. God is no puppet master. He is not going to do for us what we are quite capable of doing for ourselves. He does care, not as an interfering problem solver, but as the one who, beneath all the outer circumstances of our lives, is present challenging us to human wholeness. His guiding providence is the ground of our becoming. He is with us.

Following my brush with unreality, I have to question some areas in my spirituality. We must all do this, since our mental health is closely aligned with our spiritual condition. Nothing is so unhealthy as being involved in an unsuitable spirituality. The relationship we have to God and to religious observance must fit and perfect our personality, or we shall find ourselves in the absurdity of formalism and of trying to imitate others. When we come clear on the religious aspect of our lives we come clear on our past, and on what it is that we should be doing.

I am finding out that my spirituality has changed drastically during the nine years of my chaplaincy. From "Alone with the Alone" of the abbey, I've come to presence with little and hurting people; from "No apostolate of active service," I've come to ministry to those who will accept it; from "God on high," I've come to Christ resurrected into his people; from spirituality of Spirit only, I've come to the spirituality of what seems merely secular and material, that is, to incarnation.

There is no need to challenge the spirituality of people who live a cloistered life. It is valid. It has the blessing and approval of the Church as well as the fruits of holiness visible in its saints from the past. It is true that many cloistered people are in no way contemplative, but they help provide a setting for those who are. They have their place.

We could look at it this way: God is love. One might find one's spirituality in responding to that alone in a life of prayer and love. But there is also the reality that love is dynamic; it is always doing something. For most of us, to encounter God in his dynamic love, in his creative power, is to have our own love incarnated into action. One has to do something about it, as did the great contemplatives of the past. Or again, Christ is God. By the excellence of his divine nature he transcends all created reality. One might focus attention fully on that, bypassing, not rejecting, all created reality. But it is also true that Christ is incarnated into human reality, into his body, his people. We can find him personally present in the midst of his world. The whole of his dynamic love is revealed in the vulnerability and poverty of his loved ones. And we respond to that. This response makes historical what was only spiritual. We must all resist the temptation to private perfectionism. As Maritain pointed out, we are not called to the perfection of perfectionism, but to love perfectly while remaining very imperfect people. One must face up to the question of what kind of spirituality is ours.

Whatever the individual may think about religions, the fact is that all spiritualities are valid, and they are varied. There are Eastern, Western, Jewish, Catholic, Protestant, liturgical, charismatic and other spiritualities. One must respond to the grace one receives, and yet, at times, be caught within contrasting movements of the spirit. That is my present problem.

My problem is the egg—it is part of the ritual. One does not have a problem until one has laid a Jumbo, and it has taken on a life of its own. One can settle for having laid a Jumbo and confront the world with defiance; one can be proud of the big hole it took to lay a Jumbo; one can boast of one's ignorance as a cover up for one's refusal to learn—ignorance is a common enough commodity; one can go down fighting for one spirituality while trying to live out its opposite; one can give up the fight, feeling that the divine is ludicrous since we are merely human, or that being human is ludicrous since one man was divine. It strikes me, in something I have been reading, that Yeats, with his strange mysticism—fairies and all—accepted reality all too meekly in the end, having struggled with it all his life:

> We who still labor . . .
>> when day sinks drowned in dew,
> Being weary of the world's empires, bow down to you,
> Master of the still stars and of the flaming doors.

We have no right to escape into an individualistic contemplation just because we are weary. The empires hurt, and we shall all be dead soon enough with eternity to gaze on God, if that's the way we see it. I want to be there, to hold people's hands, to dry their tears and look into their tired eyes. But I've laid an egg, a great Jumbo egg, and no one even wants to fry it. I will pack a Jumbo for my friends. It will go to heaven and become eggs Benedict.

I have had a letter from Paulist Press accepting *Chaos* for publication. Don Brophy suggested (from the introduction) *In Praise of Chaos* for the title. I am delighted with the suggestion. It has the proper ring of the incongruous about it. I am glad that it has been accepted, but not overly excited. I would like to call up my friends and tell them, but long distance calls are discouraged. It is an occasion for celebrating; we should be going out to a restaurant and making outrageous jokes. But the day is bright and the sun is shining, and there are always ways to celebrate.

I met with my censor. His objections were few, and mostly in the area of delicacy of expression. He asked me to remove the

31

expression, "breaking wind," on the grounds that it was scatological. I gave a hoot of a laugh, and said that even "farting" was not scatological. I removed it anyway, and replaced it with "sounding off."

I sit in prayer now that "the day sinks drowned in dew." Lord, I have struggled with the questions, but I have still got that great hole in my spirit. I could curl up there, the way I see people here doubled over in a fetal position in private prayer, returned to the warmth of the womb, alone with the Alone, waiting for the great squeeze of death to bruise them out of the hole into heaven. I'll forego that. You are incarnate. We are already in heaven, only we haven't wiped our eyes. And I look across heaven, over the heads of the thousands, and I see people I care about coming toward me. They will lift me from this low seat and show me round. Amen, Lord.

6. The Basic Tensions

"I'm doing fine," we say in a time of transition, when it is perfectly clear to everybody that we are in no way doing fine. Tensions have us in their grip. Irrespective of the nature of our transition, we cannot work our way out of it without confronting the sources of our stress.

There is a tension which arises from our inability to relate the present to the future. There is nothing in our present which could indicate that anything meaningful will happen in our future. There is no comfort whatever in being told that the future is the place where the unimaginably great can happen. We have no future in which anything can happen. It is all a sick joke. We have a compelling insight that the future of which people speak is merely a mental abstraction. It is not something which in actual fact exists. We see it as a mental game people play to give purpose to their lives. But that is no longer where the purpose lies. Our integrity demands that we do not make sense of the present by playing mental games with a future which has not yet come into being. Purpose has to be experienced in the present. It is the present which must mean something. We have only today; there is no tomorrow yet. We may feel that we are drowning in the present, but we know that we have to come to grips with it. Nor should we protect ourselves against the future, fearing that what has just happened will happen again. This is a creative tension between a purposeful present and an inevitable future which is not under our control.

We can begin to deal with the tension if we acknowledge, with some measure of radical humility, that we are spiritually off balance. Without hurry or compulsion, we can work to restore the balance by bowing our head to obvious facts. We can trust that God will not lie to us, that life is always meaningful. Challenges in themselves are neither good nor bad. But a thinking person will see their purpose.

There is a tension which arises from not knowing how to express legitimate feelings. Every feeling is a good feeling: we must begin with that rule of thumb. It is what we do with it that might make it morally right or wrong. The problem is how to deal with feelings without destroying others. Anger is a legitimate feeling; it is God-given to protect us from injury. A sense of futility, of depression, of loneliness or having been unjustly treated—all are legitimate. But the tension rises because others are unable and unwilling to absorb all our feelings. The burden is too great. Their energy is all used up. There is nothing left with which to be creative or of service to others. People do, of course, affirm us, but they cannot cater to all our moods without being destroyed themselves. We are usually cast back on ourselves. All spiritual writers prescribe calm—quietly allowing the psychic pain to bring about the spiritualization of the personality, the transformation of instinct into spirit, the creation of a new interiority.

There is a tension we experience which arises from the struggle between freedom and necessity. We say that we are free, or that before we got into this transition we were free. There is some truth in that. Essentially, and deep within ourselves, we are free. But freedom is never ours as a full-blown possession. It is always intermeshed with necessity. The fact of our transition should be evidence enough of that; we did not choose to be in transition. The fact is that there are many things in our experience of living over which we have no control. This is brought painfully to our attention during transition, hence the tension.

Part of the truth about ourselves which we must realize and accept is that we are at the mercy of what is other than ourselves. Who and what we shall be is not wholly within our possession or control. This fact has to be endured with a great deal of patience. The purpose of this tension, then, is to make religious sense of this conflict between freedom and necessity. It should challenge our self-reliance and bring us into a sense of dependence on God. It humbles our godliness so that we can come clean and free before him. If this does not happen, the spiritual growth promised by transition will not take place, and we shall end up seeing ourselves as the victims of

34

irrational circumstances, or of blind fate.

This tension is greatly lessened, even if not fully resolved, by making decisions. Making a decision, any decision, is an exercise in freedom. It is a movement into God who is the ultimate goal of all our activities, whether we are aware of this or not. The freedom he gives us is not a freedom from all necessity, but a capacity to make decisions and choices which will be valid forever. The decisions need not be, as time might show, the wisest, nor need they succeed. But because they are the best we can make with the information we have, they will be the honest decisions we can stand by forever. The freedom into which we are growing is therefore forever, a capacity for the eternal. It does not mean that we shall never again be at the mercy of what is other than ourselves. It does mean that we shall be liberated one more degree from the destructiveness of those uncontrollable forces.

We shall begin to grow into this freedom once we realize that God never cuts off the conversation with his mind made up. In every event, he is unceasingly calling us into a closer union with himself. For that reason, our honest though bungling and oftentimes unwise decisions are always valid before him. The tension will cease when we finally accept the freedom of God as our freedom also and begin to act toward life from within that freedom. This is not license to do as we please, but the power to say "Yes" when yes should be said, and "No" when no should be said. Transition holds out the possibility of this freedom, the opportunity for the true transcendent self to emerge and guide our life.

Society does not always encourage this liberation. Through political propaganda, economic factors and the half-truths of the mediums of communication it demands that we act out assigned roles, play the game, wear the correct mask. Transition is a call to tear off the mask, be whole and human so as to surrender the true self to whatever God wants for the world. And society punishes those who dare to do that. See what it did to Jesus.

Tension arises then from the fact that we are scared to break free. We are tempted to suppress our truth. Transition is not always resolved in favor of accepted and conservative ways of thinking. At some point in our life we may have to make a decision which offends others—the family, Church or social group. There is considerable insecurity when we go against the grain. Society, one's peers, insecure others usually counsel adherence to accepted values. "Conform," they tell us. But to remain humanly and spiritually alive, one may not be able to conform, or at least not for a time. Conformity may be the destruction of the whole spiritual journey. It could well be a temporary and false solution.

The burdensome fact is that in transition we are always struggling with powers greater than ourselves, however we wish to name them—God, fate, unconscious instincts, people who have control of us. We find within ourselves the need to be faithful to our integrity as human persons, an integrity others cannot understand. So finding, we become locked in a struggle which will not have a clear-cut victory—others are not going to change their opinions. What victory there shall be will always be spiritual, within us rather than in the outer circumstances of our lives. In fact, a spiritual victory is inevitable because God is the ground of our living. He is with us. But we must want it. The tensions we undergo should alert us to choose the God of our future, to accept legitimate feelings, to opt for integrity, growth and inner freedom.

Routine soothes feelings and lessens tension. It even seems to enable some people to surrender their lives to God. Surrender we must, not only to God but also to life itself. Perhaps nothing very creative is expected of routine people. I feel myself being sucked into the routine here. It is an anesthetic. And in a time of transition, I feel that it is destructive. So, I am asking what it is that I should be doing with my life. Others are also asking, "Are you going to leave?"

My role in transition is moving from thoughts about the past to practical wondering about the future. One thing is certain: I shall never leave the priesthood. I ask myself if I should go back to the form of ministry I had, chaplain to some Benedictine community, or do something different such as helping a sister I know who lives and works with down-and-outs and alcoholics on skid-row in Seattle. But I am not free inside. If I leave, I want to do it in a harmony of wills with God. So far, God has not offered an opinion. He seems as distant, as silent and as inscrutable as the stars. I am torn between the need for dialogue with God and the awareness that he is so close that all dialogue is unnecessary. The thought of going to work with down-and-outs is extravagant, an enthusiasm of mine. I have no training or talent for it. But I know that I am beginning to look around.

I wonder if God has informed anybody anywhere how we should go about our transition. Perhaps we have to work our way through it alone. Perhaps it is too spiritual a journey for anybody to put words on it. I have the feeling that the message in his silence is that we are never alone, that with him transition always works itself out, that life is our own to live. Perhaps the purpose in his silence is to insist that we, being human, must take responsibility for our own lives and cease wishing it off on him. I am beginning to think that one of the purposes of transition is to enable us to change our concept of God to something more mature. Why should God have to come up with answers, handouts, bailouts—in a word, live our lives for us?

So I say to myself: "What now?" Should I stick with the great security there is here, or leave and accept the risk of being mistaken? Should I observe the enclosure as an act of faith, or leave and do some ministry? Should I stay and bury my nose in books, or leave and tell people about them? For those who are not in transition, such a decision may seem trivial, but decisions are crucial when they shape our future. Even a very small decision which has no bearing on one's future may be all-important—getting up and cooking a meal, calling a friend on the phone, walking out and looking at the flowers.

God cares. I cannot very well expect a sign. And yet, we Celtic people have baptized nature in many ways. We are always finding signs. Conversation with God has always been a normal thing for us in the language of signs: "I see his blood upon the rose,/ and in the stars the glory of his eyes. . . ." Why not? There must be some medium for dialogue. I am slow in accepting the fact that the medium of our dialogue is the silence itself, and that the fears, doubts, hopes and distress are its words. His silence compels us to know him in a way we did not understand him heretofore.

We have begun our annual retreat. I have the hope that the retreat may help me think through some aspects of transition. The routine of our life is not interrupted by it. We have two lectures daily, one in the early morning and one before retiring. It is being conducted by a young friar, and I am enjoying his observations immensely. He began by warning us that what he has to say are reflections on his own experience and on the tensions that he discovered in trying to establish a mixed—male/female—celibate community. It is all quite pleasant and relaxing, though much of it has no relationship whatever to our own way of life, and some of it is pop psychology set to religion. As retreat masters go, he is well above average.

He stressed the need for touch. That is a bit of a laugh here. In a Trappist abbey you cannot have men going around touching each other; they are much too rugged for that. Whatever be its necessity, his discussion of "skin starvation" left people still thinking they could very well survive the ordeal with their hide intact.

The pop-psych bit encourages us to focus on ourselves as a way to growth, strengthening the sagging ego. Whatever be the experience of our transition, one thing is sure: we must eventually transcend our egotism. Certainly, we have our bad moments, our self-pity, our hurt feelings, but the ultimate search is for the true deeper self, to say nothing of the search for God. If we succeed in finding God, we shall inevitably find ourselves. So we cannot afford to let our transition get bogged down. Whatever our personal concerns may be, and they are many, we have to realize that we are being called out into the open to experience life in a broader context.

Nick came by my room and we talked for an hour, a helpful break from the customary silence. He wanted to know if the retreat master was having any impact on me. I was able to tell him about all my tensions and thoughts, about God, pressure to conform and stay in the cloister, my need for some direction in my life, my commitments. I said that if I left here for the active ministry it would have to be for positive reasons, that there would be no signs other than my questions, that I would have to act in faith and not in certainty. He felt that that was all right, part of the risk in any human situation. I told him that if I acted on my own, I feared the possibility of finding myself in the wrong place. He showed me that we are never alone. I told him of my conviction that commitments should be honored. He felt that one could honor one's commitments even though the outer forms changed. He was good, putting his finger on the real issues. He, the abbot, my friends all think that I should get out of here. I hesitate, partly because I have always idealized this uncompromising way of life, partly because of some rigid elements in my feelings that surface strange fears. The whole thing is irrational, but, then, if it were logical I would not be in transition.

I sit in prayer before I retire, my tensions, feelings and questions cast aside like a heap of clumsy clothes. Tomorrow will be time enough to wear them again.

I ask God to cast all fear out of my mind by the power of his love. I ask him to bring my head and my heart into harmony again.

I pray for others, for women who fear leaving brutal husbands, for men who fear leaving work that endangers their health, for parents unable to let go of their children. I pray for the whole irrational situation, because in the end I know that all prayer is answered.

7. Killing the Snake

The empty center, the depths, the vault, the demonic state—the arrogant assertions—resound and reverberate in the hollow man, the man in transition.

I had a terrifying dream which must mean something of importance: "There is a woman whose daughter is supposed to be picked up by another woman. The other woman has not received the message because the phone is on the answering service. I realize immediately that the young daughter is in great danger of being swallowed by the snake. I get a shovel and rush to the place where she was, hoping to save her. When I get there, the snake, a huge python, has crushed and swallowed her. The snake is enormous, its head lifted up to the level of my chest. I swing with the shovel in rage, and keep hacking and hacking until I have completely hacked its head off. Inside the neck are seeds of some kind. Somebody has arrived and is opening the snake and removing the dead body. I have my back to it and will not turn and look."

There is a knot inside me that gets tighter and tighter. Just for relief, I shall probably make some stupid decision. I call the decision stupid because I do not want to take a step that may later have to be reversed.

This, I think, is what my problem is about: those of us who are in transition have, to a greater or lesser degree, been burnt. We do not want that to happen again. We are, of course, over-cautious. But we have small bits of wisdom itemized in our minds. We are aware that the reality we do not know is vastly greater than the reality we know.

We have a distrust of partial knowing. It was partial knowing which got us into this. And we have a distrust of the calm assumption of wisdom which our advisors display, fearing that any claim to a superior wisdom will block whatever insight our concrete situation needs. The fact is that we should like to be safe and secure again. We look for some stability again. We feel that there are very few ways of getting back to that stability, perhaps only one, but there are thousands of ways of getting burnt again. We want our decision, when we make it, to be the apt and only possible one. We are stubborn about that.

I have a block inside which prevents me from seeing, at this time in my life, any purpose to my being here. So I fear that from my blockheadedness will flow some inept course of action. Yet, decisions have to be made. Getting people in transition to make decisions is a major endeavor. We are in the grip of emptiness and distrust. We have only our dreams.

Our dreams are not all nightmares. We daydream about a real good, our future well-being, but we think of it in ways that are sentimental, a sort of vain enthusiasm. There is also a real evil which drives us to a sense of defeat and spiritual despair. This sense of defeat makes us feel that we can do nothing. We are discovering that evil really is evil, and that it is a defeat within a person who has given up the will to live. It is an enclosure within oneself where one is isolated from others and from reality. But good really is good, and there is nothing vain or sentimental about it. It is a power to transcend our selfishness. We are fundamentally good, if flawed, persons, and in our transition we are called to be better.

Making a decision is risky for this reason: that the human heart is ambivalent to both good and evil, now allured by one, now by the other. We are capable of unpredictable deeds of selfishness as well as of generosity. We always act within some risk; it is the human condition and is perfectly all right. But the evil, with its defeat and despair, is exposed and overcome by the pain we experience in transition when we allow that pain to touch us. We are not the victims of fate but the creators, through our decisions, of our own destiny. This state of fearfulness and risk is not an occasion for either defeat or vain optimism. If anything, it is a time for discernment.

I talked to the abbot. He was most understanding. He said that I should have the inner authority and freedom to go, if I felt that is what I should do. It reminded me of my theologian-friend's insistance that one must exercise inner authority, that is, be the author of one's personal response to God. The abbot said, "If it means anything to you, you have my permission to go or to stay as you see fit." It does mean much to me, but I still have to take responsibility for my life and my decisions. That, I cannot wish off on anybody, not even on God. I am, however, appreciative of the abbot's breadth of view.

It happens all too often that people in authority abuse their power by making it an instrument of control, rather than of ministry. Authority mediates the personal betterment of others, what God is calling them to do and be. If it fails to accomplish that, it must either be tyrannical, a form of coercion, or government by baby talk—an effective form of mind control with which nobody can come to grips. The proper use of leadership in the Church persuades, supports and demands involvement. It respects the essential dignity, equality and freedom of decision of others. I am fortunate in having found this form of authority here. And it is my hope that when people in transition experience clerical coercion when they seek direction, they will have no scruple in walking away from it.

I thought these things over for a few days and finally came to a decision. I wrote to the sister I know in Seattle to see if she has a job for me. If she says "Yes," I shall leave here. In any event, I have decided that I must seek the face of God elsewhere, and serve him in others. It is a decision I make in the reality of being at his disposal.

The snake came back again. It was neither friendly nor unfriendly: "I find myself in the bottom clositer of the abbey with a huge fifty foot long python. I am at its tail, but its head is lifted up and looks back at me with large glittering eyes. Someone is with me. He has taken an old shotgun from the wall and fires two shots, trying to blast its head off. He misses. I know that he is not aiming carefully. I leave the building, and from the outside hear two more shots. I know that he has missed again. I have the feeling that the snake can follow my tracks, so I decide to go away somewhere. I think I know where I am going. I find myself driving in heavy traffic, but the road is narrow and the traffic will not move over. Now I am walking. I am consulting a map, but the map is not clear. I am getting into some wilderness area. At this point I slip off the road and hang clinging to its edge. The edge is smooth rock and clinging to it is difficult. Down, miles below me, I can see a valley with fields and trees. I am hanging from the edge of a cliff. People are passing back and forth above me. I long for one of them to reach a hand to me, but nobody does so. Weakness passes all over my body, and I know that if I pass out I shall fall. I put my head down on my arm to rest."

The bell for rising rang, and I woke up with a bad headache. I know that the battle between freedom and necessity is far from finished.

I went to church, and there was a reading in the morning praise about Gideon looking for a sign. God told him, "Peace be with you; have no fear; you will not die" (Judges 6:22). And the symbol of the rock came up a few times in the psalms; "I have placed your feet upon a rock." I appreciated those readings, although I felt that my feet were falling off the rock. It is a strange thing, but I have noticed that when we actually get some small sign from God—the synchronicity of things—we do not always trust it, or, more aptly, we do not trust God.

I ran into one of our monks, a Jungian psychologist who studied at Zurich, and told him about the snake thing. "Wow," he said, "you're really suppressing it." We made an appointment to discuss snakes.

Thinking about thinking is bad business, and reflecting about doing is not much better. Perhaps it is a curse that comes from writing. Then again, who wants to be a performing zombie? Years ago I would have considered it a great imperfection: praying and knowing that I was praying. Now that I feel somewhat lost, my life quite confused, it does not seem to matter much. I am not sure that getting lost in prayer, or work, or study, or writing is much of a virtue. It would be good to think that it is in God, or in his will, that I am lost and not in the outer darkness. But reflecting on it brings this clear attitude: I have no difficulty in appreciating that everybody else is saved. It is a satisfactory experience. And I reflect that so often when people are quite sure that they are saved they go about preaching: "Brother, repent, or you will go to hell." I would rather stay with the first experience.

In a time of transition it is very easy to give up on God, precisely because it is easy to give up on ourselves. But we have to struggle through with God somehow, not an abstract God but the God who got himself crucified. Whatever be our distress, there is no way we can belittle a God who has been flogged and nailed up to die. We may think we are in bad shape, but the simple truth is that we were in far worse shape when we lived complacent, unquestioning lives. As a woman whose husband died put it to me on one occasion, "Comfort is the enemy of growth."

I have been candling the eggs. They come in two rows down a small ramp from the left, and roll over a series of lights which glow through them. I watch eight of them at a time as I sit in a dark box-like place. Those which are cracked or have blood spots have to be removed. The spot of blood is dark and whirls around inside the shell as the egg rolls past. It has a satellite existence of its own. I get one chance to see it, and if it is missed some housewife will surely get disgusted as she breaks it onto her frying pan. Someone around here was in the habit of saying to people who complained about this that a blood spot was the sign of a high protein egg. Like the evening news, everybody felt that bit of nonsense very satisfying. It answered everything.

The eggs roll on past me to a machine which separates them according to size. The machine has a repeated clickety-clack refrain which seems to say over and over, "Inward theology, inward theology, inward theology." One each "inward" the eggs roll and stop, roll and stop, roll and stop. I translate the sounds and movement into the ritual of transition. I think of how people in transition are the ones who are acutely aware of what inward theology is really about. It is what people do when all the theological tomes are silent with regard to the heartbreaks of life, when people have to find a personal God in their own personal way. Many of them have told me what this inward theologizing is, and I quote them: "Finding it difficult to forgive God," "Trusting in God when I was torn apart inside," "Praying and coming to know the truth I did not want to face," "Driving alone and crying and asking God 'Why?' " It is the theology which life teaches us, and in the end it is the theology we trust. In this inward way we come to know that God is alive and that he cares. Parents should surely be aware of this when they complain that the children are not being taught the basics. "Religion is life," my niece Sheila used to lisp when she was five years old. Someone had taught her that, but who can teach us what life is?

44

I went over to the feed-lot with Nick after candling eggs one day. He had a young vet up to work on a couple of cows that had cancer on their eyes. It was not good for one's stomach. We drove the cows into a couple of chutes and clamped them tightly with only their heads free. They bawled and moaned in an almost human manner as we put clamps in their noses, pulled their heads sideways and tied them in position.

The first operation was not so bad. The vet froze the growth off with liquid nitrogen. The second had the cancer on the eyeball itself. After anesthetizing the area, he tried to pop the eye out of the socket so as to work more easily on it. He did not succeed and did some damage to the eye. At that point he decided to cut the eye out altogether, a not infrequent operation. That I did not have to take. I left. At least a cow cannot reflect on what is happening to her. I wonder if God reflects on it. Does he have a secret wisdom about cows that escapes us? "Who can know the mind of God?"

But I want to know the mind of our Jungian monk. He shall be my St. Patrick and cast the snakes out of my Irish soul.

I sit in the dark to pray to God, my feet crossed, my back to the wall. I tell God that I continue to be in a tight place, caught between the army and the sea.

I tell him that since childhood I have always believed that if ever I got into such a situation, he would reach down and snatch me out of there. I do not see him doing that. There is a moment of silence. Then, I hear the words inside me:

"Swim, you poor bastard, swim!"

"But I'll drown."

"Of course you'll drown. But, then again, you just might survive."

With my mind fixed on being rescued, I was not, until now, able to hear the real message.

"Amen, Lord."

45

8. Snake Oil and Salvation

There is a patience which accepts suffering because of weakness and poor self-image. It perpetuates evil and is sterile. There is a patience in which we accept our humanness with humble sincerity. It faces us up to our real truth, that is, to what God thinks of us. It opens up our thinking and brings us together in creative love.

I spent an hour with our monk psychologist and his insights from Jung. We poured snake oil on troubled waters. Although it was good, a positive talk, it had too much of "It could be this or it could be that." The snake is what I am repressing; most people in transition repress something. The seeds are those of future creativity, provided I cease trying to kill the snake. I have to make peace with it.

It seems that cliff-hanging is perfectly acceptable. It is as good a definition of transition as any other. It would be quite another matter if one were casting oneself off the cliff. On the other hand, it might indicate a fear of going down into the unconscious, but down there is a fertile valley. The seeds of everything that is creative are sown in the unconscious. The snake is an old-time symbol of creative activity, of life and fertility. But if one's creativity is frustrated, locked in the unconscious without opportunity for sharing, the snake becomes something to fear. It devours one. I resent that with fury and break open the unconscious. In the process come to life seeds of future service. Afterward I feel relieved. But the snake never attacks me. It is sufficient for it to be there. It is feared for the power it has, and revered (in past ages, worshiped) for the source of creativity it symbolizes.

But there are other fears we have, arising from the way we were taught in our youth to fear the God who, supposedly, punishes those who do not conform. I counsel others in this matter and have no problem. I do not do a very good job of counseling myself. God is the God of love. I can see in others the call to inner freedom, creativity and growth. All I can reach for within myself is a measure of patient sincerity.

Religious fear is a disastrous heritage. Many of us still have it, and one good effect of this spiritual journey will be to grow out of it. A friend of mine spent some time with me before I returned to the abbey. He was going through an unpleasant transitional period and needed to talk. As he saw it, one could not be free until one had disposed of the whole bag of tricks—religion, image, concept of God. He cited Eckhart, James Joyce and Merton amongst others. I had difficulty getting the feel of his thought, knowing that it was his own mongrel of false images he was trying to abandon. Now, I think, I can understand him a little better.

People like ourselves who come out of a religious fear background have to go through a radical change before we can grasp what salvation is all about. We have to be able to see damnation as an accomplishment before we can see salvation as a gift. In our youth we were given to understand that salvation was the accomplishment, that if we performed well and conformed we could earn heaven. What really was being said there was that we did not need Christ, that we could save ourselves. But we found out that performance was possible only up to a point. We could never satisfactorily do it. So guilt and damnation dogged our steps. There was always somebody there who made sure we knew how wrong we were. The moral theologians mongrelized us. We were hardly free to do good because we were so preoccupied with evil. We were not taught that salvation was a gift, that it was damnation—the ultimate expression of isolation from others—which was the accomplishment, and a difficult one at that. This sort of problem becomes acute in a time of transition because we sense the presence of evil in feelings of defeat, worthlessness, rejection and isolation.

I have come to know people who are far more fatalistic than I am. After all, the Irish mind is too mercurial to make a career out of despair. I have tried at times, usually in homilies, to lift the burden and offer a freedom image of God. Those of a one track mind would have no part of it. They would have the oppression that came with legalistic thinking in preference to the responsibility that came with freedom. I am thinking, of course, of a mature spiritual freedom, not of license to do as one pleases. We like security, but it is an illusion. Conform, and everything will be in control. But now, in this spiritual journey of transition, we are called beyond that to love. And there is risk in loving, and especially in loving God. Salvation has to be accepted as one of the gifts of love. It is the mystery of the incomprehensible God of love and freedom welling up within our own love and freedom. If that is not allowed to happen, we sooner or later become devoured by our inner snakes.

The way out of the impasse is not easy. What I offered people in homilies were only ideas. Ideas do not help very much because they are only things. Simone Weil writes that one does not give things to the afflicted, or do things for them. What one must do is give oneself, project one's "self" into them, so that for a little while one restores to them what they have lost, a sense of their own identity. My friends had the power to do that for me—teasing, laughing, sharing, refusing to accept false ideas: "You know, Sean, you have to be careful . . . Jeez, I don't know how to put this . . . you know, about the way you think of salvation." "Yeh, yeh, you don't have to be apologetic."

Our retreat continues. The happy friar (he looks a little like Brer Rabbit) said that celibates who could live as celibates and not be in love, and in the happiness of being in love (he sounded very autobiochemical), were not true celibates, because their witness was no more than that of crusty bachelors or sour old maids. The expression "being in love" bothers me as being somewhat too superficial. Who would expect people in transition—divorcees, hospital patients, rest home inmates, widows and widowers—to be in the happiness of being in love? Christ had no greater love than when he laid down his life for his friends, and I don't know that being happy about it was required of him. Ideals are all very fine, but real life is just not established by grinning celibates. Much of what contributes to human happiness—conversations (the universal recreation), sharing one's life, going places, doing things with others—is very frequently not possible for those in transition. Nor does it mean that the essential value of their life is lessened. It is a time of learning a new depth. There might be happiness in isolated moments of prayer, in study and in the beauties of nature. But what transitional people want is courage.

Brer Friar has a theology about being celibate, charitable and chaste that is uproariously entertaining. Even the most dour amongst the brethren have a good-natured, if stunned, look on their faces. He maintains that the purpose of religious life—speaking from his considerable experience—is to fall in love (upraised eyebrows). It is a balancing act, he continues, between charity and chastity. Too much charity is not good for you, because you are apt to lose your chastity (sharp intake of breath); too much chastity is not good for you, because you are apt to become grumpy and lose your charity (amazed disblief). If you are all chaste and charitable, he says, you no longer need God and have wound up in the sin of being your own savior. If you are neither chaste nor charitable—brother, you're damned! Struggle, he maintains, is the answer. The thing is to struggle with both and learn to trust a loving Father. God uses human weakness, he gushed, to rush toward people and gather them into his arms. Ugh! I don't know. Christ must always come first. We have to love deeply and universally and let people "be," for the love of God. Maybe that is smug.

I found a little book by Merton that is helpful, *Life and Holiness*. He writes: "The love of God is a preference, and therefore demands sacrifice." "To be perfect as Christ is perfect we must be as perfectly human as he." Merton also writes: "Sanctity is not a question of being less human but of being more human than others." That is salvation, and it will take more than snake oil to bring it about.

I feel that we have anchored our ship somewhere in space. We are marooned. But not to worry, not to worry at all—we have all our lives to live here. There is no urgency. Yet, these men are a sign, a sort of collective sacramental sign to others in this part of the country of the reality and absolute claim of God. One may discuss religion for all time provided one uses only words and ideas, but when a group of men witness with their lives and refuse to argue, it is a pretty insuperable demonstration of faith. I have been thinking that what is being done here in night vigils in praise of God is as valid as what is being done in Night Watch with the alcoholics and street people in Seattle. That also is a way of praising God.

I feel completely detached from whatever reply I get from there. Either way, "Yes" or "No," will be God's providence. Now that I have let go of damnation, I feel that God and I have both let go of our trapezes, each thinking the other was the one to have held on. Now I know that salvation is a gift of God's own holiness. And that can never be ours as being "of" us. There is purpose in our feeling of rejection, or in the feeling that God does not care, and it is that there is a gulf between who we are and who God is that we are beginning to acknowledge. This does not imply separation. On the contrary, it is his presence which enables us to recognize who he is, the Holy One, the Savior. It enables us to accept our created humanness with humility and sincerity.

I went over to the guest house and met a holy little man. He has none of the pretensions or the cultural varnish of consciously religious people. He had been an alcoholic for years, but has sobered up. He drinks gallons of coffee. I sat and drank with him. I asked him if he had been married. He told me that he had been, but his wife of only a year and a half died. That was forty years ago. He went to pieces. Some months later his relatives found him in a flop house in Chicago. He went from skidrow to skidrow across the country for the rest of his life. Now he lives in an unfurnished apartment, existing on minimal social security. He is a wounded gentle person. I spoke to him of meeting his young wife again, of the joy and celebration that are still ahead, of making up for lost time. He looked up from his coffee with sad eyes and nodded. I have the feeling that his transition is completed.

I sit in prayer with people in transition.

Lord, through no choice of ours, we have been called into struggle with the condition of things as we knew them. We wish to end this present condition, not selfishly, but in the fullness of what you have planned for us, in the saving that is your love for us.

We do not wish to bend reality, or control it, but to become the reality of our deepest truth, that which you think of us. We wish to know your freedom at the center of who we are and to stand by that freedom.

We feel that we are strangers to you, and yet we know that we are at home with you. Amen.

50

9. Prayer and Another Enthusiasm

God, in cloud or light, destroys our petty understanding and challenges us to live trustingly with him, only to challenge us further if we survive. Try as we might to comprehend, he will always overwhelm us unexpectedly with dismay or with delight.

We must expect our prayer to be in a very strange place during a time of spiritual growth. We have the feeling of being abandoned by God—not overlooked but positively rejected. How, we ask, can we relate to God when more and more we do not understand him? It is impossible for us to get a grasp on what is going on. We wish there were someone who could begin at the beginning and explain to us all about God. We have the growing feeling that all we understood in the past was childish. What we know of God is always filtered through our personalities (we know Christ by becoming Christlike), and when our personalities are involved in transition the whole question of God is challenged. There are, of course, certain abstract statements about religion which we accept, but what we are seeking is a live interaction with an alive God.

This is a crucial time when many people in transition either blame God for their difficulties, as if he were some kind of public servant, or blame the Chrch, or get sour and cynical about religion. People drift in disillusionment from what, in fact, was never true, to disgust and, finally, to disinterest. Yet, much of that is childish pouting, the refusal of the challenge to growth and maturity.

Who is this person we call G-O-D? We cannot possibly know him as we know other people and objects. We know him, not by grasping him and surrounding him in our minds as an object of

51

knowledge, but by being grasped by him in some mysterious way in the depths of our spirit. Our approach to God is always a response made in faith, knowing him by being known by him. We are haunted by him, approaching him when we are called past all finite things to listen to his silence. We need the courage to accept God's self-emptying (Phil. 2:2-8) as our way also, the transformation of all that is little, and weak, and poor in spirit into his body. Coming closer to this mystery of God is part also of our spiritual journey in transition.

As for his being "Almighty," everyone, except those who love power and control, knows that there is nothing mighty about him. What is unique about him is that he shares our own powerlessness. I wonder how much the militarism of Israel had to do with coining that name for him, the God of Armies. We've had Gideon's and Abimelech's atrocities for our reading in church with the psalmist trampling down his enemies. It sickens me, like something the military governments of today would write. Yes, of course, God is the absolute power which sustains the universe from vanishing into nothingness, and yes, he has already destroyed the power of evil. But his power is that of love. It is paradoxical, the power of a crucified man who forgave his murderers. Perhaps we should be concerned with doing something for him, rather than waiting for him to do something for us. The facts of the case are that in our transition we are being called into a likeness to this God who does not cease loving.

For all our words, it is we who are addressed by God, and not God who is addressed by us. The moment we try to make him public servant number one, we try to manipulate him. And that is magic. We would benefit by remaining silent in his presence. But it should be a positive silence, a concentrated attention. The theory which maintained that a vacuum of the mind in prayer would automatically be filled by God has no evidence to sustain it. A vacuum of the mind, like any other vacuum, is quite capable of picking up whatever trash comes its way. God does not do anything automatically, especially fill empty minds. A mind full of silent attention is not empty; it is in a state of alertness to whatever God has to say.

I had a strange experience in prayer today. I had better explain. Experiences are second guesses. They are entirely of our own making. It is a translation of something spiritual that is happening to us into a symbol we can understand with our senses, or upon which we can reflect. The experience is not, therefore, the essential grace of prayer, nor its essential content. It is secondary. Since it is of our own doing, the work of our creative imagination, it is of itself unimportant, though it enlightens us. Such experiences are frequently displeasing to others who feel they are dishonestly or willfully invented.

This experience was a deeper awareness of what I had understood when I asked, "What if togetherness could not die on the cross?" I seemed to see the face of Christ so vividly imprinted on my imagination that, try as I might, I could not turn away from it. It was the face of a crucified old man, a man two thousand years old. He was not able to die because he continues to be crucified in his people, his body, until the end of time. I saw that asking a crucified old man for help was all wrong. He was asking me for help. He could not die because love cannot die. He would be togetherness, the God of total surrender to his people until the end of time. He is the power in the powerlessness that never ceases to trust, the silence in all who are unable or unwilling to defend themselves, the inarticulate in all the little ones. Already, the transformation of the world, the reign of God in the hearts of the poor in spirit, is taking place. There is Easter joy in that. But in what it costs the little ones, there are two thousand years of sadness. I think I have caught a glimpse of both.

Coming out of my new awareness of Christ is a new joy. For today, at least, I am really happy, full of the joy of the Lord. Whole new areas have opened up inside me.

I whistled to myself while packing eggs, the whistling covered by the noise of the machinery—Waltzing Matilda, some Borodin, something from Tchaikovsky, all having to do with dancing. I packed a Jumbo for my friends because I seem to have come out of that empty place inside me, not into heaven yet, but more alive on earth.

But I daydreamed, also. I found myself having a second enthusiasm. Since I have already written to the sister in Seattle, this bothers me as a sort of betrayal. If I am sincere about working with down-and-outs, why am I now thinking of something else? I am daydreaming (romanticizing, really) about some form of monasticism which would be available to the poor, a slum monasticism. I am well aware of the fact of not having a talent to organize such a venture. But I seem to see the necessity of it. It should be lay, not clerical, with commitments for a year at a time. That would provide for those who might find themselves unable to make a lifetime commitment. It could be formed around a nucleus of people who had vows. It would be celibate for those who lived together, but open in every other way for the participation of married couples. It could be supported by the part-time labor of those who had jobs in the secular sphere. This would leave time for study, prayer and service to others. The primary demand would be that people live together in Christian charity. Too many experimental groups were founded and failed because they excluded people they disliked. The urban monasticism which now exists is too encrusted with law and tradition, too identified with the prevailing culture. The Benedictine sisters are beginning to do something. It will be of interest to see how far they go. The love of learning, liturgy, art and music could go a long way toward making the city desert bloom.

I came across an article written by Merton for the *Journal of Ecumenical Studies*, November, 1967. These same ideas are presented there. However, on page 160 of his *Conjectures of a Guilty Bystander*, he writes about how a Colombian novice came to him after the liturgy on Holy Thursday and asked him why he could not come to Colombia and found a form of monasticism which would appeal to modern people. Merton wrote that he could not tell the novice (why not?) how much he would like to do that, but that it would mean that he would have to leave the Order and Gethsemani, and he would never do that. What strikes me is this: if he wanted to do it, and if he were capable of doing it, why could he not go ahead? Was it just the spirit of the time, or the power of his abbot, which prevented him? If it had not been a nobody novice, but the Pope who had asked him, he would have been out of there like a shot. That is the kernel of what we miss. God speaks on Holy Thursday through the mouth of a novice, the need being there and the Pope being absent, and he is not heard because of his powerlessness.

There is little lost in daydreaming. There are enough discordant elements in such a project to sober anyone up. I search for the source of my daydreaming—a vain and sentimental enthusiasm, or a mild megalomania? One of the realities of enclosure, to say nothing of being in a time of transition, is that the mind expands in fantasies which are as easily destructive as constructive. God does not want things quite the same way as we want them. At the most, his Spirit is on occasions active within our spirit. Those are times for discernment. When we people in transition recognize these half-irrational, but compulsive, enthusiasms for new and great achievements, we should slow down and listen to another person's opinion. Still, any enthusiasm is better than giving in to a sense of worthlessness. We are never worthless.

My thoughts lead me to reflect on the purpose in life of people who lead a cloistered life. My admiration for them has little to do with their prayer lives. There are people of prayer everywhere, and the prayer life is not all that exalted in every individual cloistered person. What I admire is the generosity with which they squander their lives, gambling them away on an act of pure faith. I am sure that they will be rewarded for their witness. But the temptation in the cloistered life is to make this squandering meaningful by attempts to justify it. The offering of one's life does not have to be justified, nor does the act of faith have to be reduced to reasons that are self-evident. Both faith and the offering transcend all that is of mere reason.

There is no need for them to try to be meaningful. Any such attempt is illusory. Saying that they are contemplatives does not make them understandable; searching for reasons which might make them relevant for today's society does not make them relevant. There is no need to say or prove anything, unless they wish to say that they are fools for Christ's sake. Perhaps most of them say even that. These people have given up their freedom of mobility and their relevance for a self-serving world in an outlandish act of faith. And they are normal people, not drop-outs, nor fanatics, nor pseudo mystics. Those who criticize them for running away from the responsibilities of the world would think twice of it had they to live amongst them. Nor are such critics willing to make a gift of their own lives in any like degree. If it were that easy to avoid responsibility, the abbeys would be bursting at the seams. They are not. In some respects, these people are the world's most radically responsible ones.

The true relevance of cloistered people for our world of nuclear blackmail is to divest themselves of all image making and image keeping. All attempts at establishing credibility should be rejected. They have about as much credibility as a man named Jesus, executed as a counter-culture troublemaker. They should rejoice when they are scorned, for then they are true solitaries. Those of us who wish to work in the active ministry have our own solitude, knowing that we save nobody. God does that. At most we uncover what is already theirs. We also seek the face of God where it is revealed to us.

I pray before retiring.

Once more, with surprising emphasis, I have a sense of God's remoteness and aloofness, his absolute silence. His silence is destroying my vanity. I resist that happening, but until it happens my true self will not emerge.

I ask for assurance that what I am doing is correct. But there is no need for that. The kind of certitude I seek is only found in things which can be assessed and measured, finite things. God cannot be measured.

Lord, grant me fidelity to your promise of love. Do not allow me to submit you to something finite, to some psychological certitude. That would reduce my longing to magic. Putting my trust in such comfort is idolatry.

I trust absolutely that you are, and that you are loving. Let me be at your disposal as Christ was. Let me say "Amen" to his way of life. Amen.

10. The Journey Deepens

If we lose heart in the middle of our transition, there will be nothing for it but to pull back into the security of an underdeveloped life. We may never get the opportunity to grow again. But if we stand up to God, he will swallow us alive.

During the time of our transition we could profit greatly from having someone close to us to whom we could speak freely. This is seldom possible, and, failing it, prayer is a vital necessity. It is remarkable how things come clear in prayer, even if in a paradoxical manner.

We should realize that were we not aware of God in some obscure but very true fashion, we could not possibly be aware of his silence. It is knowing by unknowing. Rather than try to manipulate God, we have to leave him absolutely free in our regard, something he is going to be whether we like it or not. His silence is more than ours, but it is ours also. It is the silence of all God's poor. It is not the silence of indifference, of anger, or of pouting. It is the silence that confronts the reality of our world, the silence of those who have been so hurt that, in fact, nothing comes to mind to say. The burden of that human condition has been placed on the shoulders of all who are in transition. The spiritual journey is made in solidarity with all God's people. We experience the tragedy of all things finite. We cannot opt out of our relationship to them. But it is precisely because in some vast, though obscure way, we have compassion for the frailty of the finite that we sense the infinity of the Infinite.

This seeming silence of God is the silence of Jesus before Pilate,

of those who don't know "anyone" in high places

of the poor before the wealthy, of the powerless before the powerful, of our own brokenness before our limitless destiny.) With the contemplative dimension of our spirit we have to deepen our insertion into all who are poor and finite and find God in that place. God's silence is that of those who have no words left, no thoughts, no ideas, and we have to accept that. In the temple of the poor in spirit, God is indeed a very silent Spirit.

I came across an article on the discernment of spirits by Hans Urs von Balthasar which is very helpful. It can be found in the Fall 1980 issue of *Communio: International Catholic Review*. It is very meaty from a theological point of view, and helpful on the question of discernment. He writes: "Wherever the relationship of the finite to the infinite has been thought through with any kind of purity and consistency, we always find an approach to knowledge of the divine on the way of negation . . . in place of grasping, a letting loose of every will to comprehend in order to let oneself be grasped." Also, "The one who is spiritually spontaneous is the one who lives also in continuous receptivity. . . ." The article affirms what in stumbling fashion we do during transition. It does not deal with discernment from a technical or psychological point of view, but bases it on the theology of the Trinity. It explains the difference of approach of the active apostolic worker to the poor—protest, organizations, projects, political action—and that of the concerned contemplative presence: entering spiritually into the experience, seeing the face of the crucified Christ there, having compassion for them, uncovering their deepest beauty. Vision complements action, and prayer becomes an energy center for change in the world.

I can see now that our concept of God, which is always partial, fashions the response we make to him, our life style. And our response, the way we live, reinforces our concept. For example: if our concept of God is that of the Wholly Other, Transcendent Mystery, an unusual concept in today's theology, one might be moved to respond to this by attempts to transcend all created things—leave the world, as we say. One might enter a cloistered community. But if one's concept is that of God incarnated into his people and resurrected into personal presence to them, one's response would be to seek and find God there. Should a person consider liberation theology as the most relevant expression of thought about things of God, it is unlikely that one's response would move one to enter a

Trappist abbey. In a Trappist abbey, liberation theology can never be more than a hobby.

There is something of the active and the contemplative in every person, the active person being contemplative to the extent that ministry is more than social welfare alone. There is the Gospel dimension. But the cloistered person must not hoard the gifts he has received or he will find himself preoccupied by very petty concerns. The silence of God in a time of transition humbles us enough to convince us that we do not have many answers, that we need to broaden our concept of God.

Nick came by with a copy of *The Catholic Agitator*, the October 1980 issue. It is a publication of the Los Angeles Catholic Workers group. He laughed and said that the title alone would be enough to scare the pants off most of the men in this place (actually, monks do not wear pants under the habit, just long-johns, which makes their feet seem so large). The issue is devoted to *Resistance and Contemplation*. The lead article, written by a Trident protester, challenged the monks for having made their peace with the world. He pointed to the monks of the Egyptian and Syrian deserts of the early Church, and called on present day monks to be on the margins again, running counter to the world's insane preoccupation with self-destruction. The courts protect militarism, he says, because they see it as the only option for survival in today's world. He asks the monks to come up with a better option.

Perhaps there are some who are doing just that, the ten just men, so to speak, who are saving the city. There is a mystical dimension that he may be missing, a very real and functional one, an identification and union with the poor and the peacemakers that a genuine monk would have from his insertion into the body of Christ. It might be quite as effective, and at times vastly more demanding, than physical presence and protest.

My thoughts turn to my brothers here. Who are they? What do I see? They are not "a collection of private wildernesses." They are a collection of fertile oases surrounded by desert, true solitaries. Each is personally fruitful—one can see it in their peacefulness—and each has a wall surrounding himself, his solitariness, to keep the desert out. I wander round this desert, going from oasis to oasis, pausing to look within. Only Nick invites me in. But I cannot cease wandering lest I become a heap of rocks in the wasteland and fit in well with the landscape. Already, I fit in too well. I walk quietly, observe the silence for the most part, do my chores, play my part in the ritual. "You are fitting in so nicely," said our local Thomist to me the other day, and I gave a snort of a laugh. We were on our way into the kitchen to pick up supper.

People were ladling out bowls of celery soup. I declined the soup and created a magnificent salad from meager resources, dressing it in French. While admiring the opulence of it all—the salivary glands tightening under my jaws with anticipation—the whole thing fell on the tile floor with a Klaxon ring from my metal plate. It was ego consuming. The novice master and a novice helped me clean up the oily mess. But several seemed not amused. Could it be from my having fatalistically and loudly exclaimed: "Oh, feces!" or words to that effect?

It is time to pray. I ask the Father, in the name of his Son, to grant me his Spirit. I put myself in a state of total emptiness before him—emptiness of ideas, images and requests. It is a bit of a struggle at first, holding my silence up to him. I let go of everything, even of receiving, and try to enter his rest. I let go of the past, the good and the bad of it, and my future, my staying or leaving here. I drop this moment of time, this little bit of space. I let go of my ego identity.

A huge dark hole, a bottomless void, opens up before me. I fall into it with a sense of terror and dread. Waves of dread go over me. I am falling through nothingness, and will go on falling for eternity. I am falling through eternal being—there is no doing. I have to trust blindly that this void is God, trust his benevolence, trust that the void is goodness. Dying might be like this, but I am not dying, nor am I having an emotional problem. I am merely letting go, releasing plans and hopes, myself and my future. At the end I know that we do not, any of us, belong to ourselves. We belong to God. I know also that our futures and our "selves," should we ever surrender our ego-image, myth-mask, belong to him, not in mindless slavery but in covenant love.

The falling ends and I find myself in another of those vivid imaginative, spiritual-translation, experiences. I am standing on a sandy beach before the ocean, a symbol for God. The entire ocean comes toward me and encircles me. It enters me and passes out through eyes, mouth and hands. The whole movement of God

60

continues in one silent flow. I recall something I had written in *In Praise of Chaos* about going the long way home by way of the ocean. I see that the silences are the mystery as well as the weaknesses of all of us, that they are no obstacle to God. My prayer ends, and I open my eyes. Something has changed. *Is this how to bring about change in oneself?*

God gives the totality of himself to us uninterruptedly. His essence is surrender; nothing is held back. We are loved into continuing existence by an absolute love. We are loved for our own sakes, and not for our performance. In this spiritual journey of our transition we are called to a like surrender and to a like love. When both surrenders meet there is light, love and understanding. There is life to the full, God's life, which is eternal, offered in time. Amen to that.

11. The Failure of Enthusiasms

God has not offered us a job to do in life; he has offered us a covenant of love to fulfill. That covenant can be fulfilled even when all jobs fail.

I had a dream, and I am wondering if it is telling me something: "I am up to my waist in the ocean, about a half-mile out from the shore. I am carrying a child on my arm, and trying to get to land. There is a boatful of people next to me but I do not want to get into the boat. A violent storm has come up on the ocean between me and the shore. The bottom of the ocean begins to slope down toward the shore, and a voice says to me, "Do not go down there, or you will be drowned.'"

On the feast of our Cistercian (Trappist is a nickname) founders, Saints Robert, Alberic and Stephen, I expected God to do something dramatic in my life. I can't quite get away from the idea that God is dramatic—this despite the fact that experience proves the opposite. Still, with my peculiar mix of theology, faith, spirituality and vision, I trust "the God of seldom surprises." Robert of Molesme, our chief founder, was an extraordinary seeker after God—easily, in the externals, the most unstable founder there ever was. But within himself, he was altogether stable in seeking God's face.

Robert entered his first abbey at the age of fifteen, was some time later chosen leader of a second, but left there to return to the first. He was then appointed prior of a third and, not getting along well with the community, left there to join a group of hermits—his fourth house. He brought the hermits with him to found a fifth, the abbey of Molesme. He left Molesme with his prior, Alberic, with

Stephen Harding, an Englishman, and a group of others, to found his sixth, Citeaux, the motherhouse of the Cistercian order. The year was 1098. After some time, he was ordered by Rome to return to Molesme, and it was there that he died.

Any thinking person can see that the *gratia capitis*, the overall grace of leadership, which was given to Robert, combined a very stable search for God within a very unstable outer life. It might be quite in keeping with the founder for one of his followers to have a searching spirit within a wandering body. Undoubtedly he was driven by the knowledge that the limits of one's vocation into God are never reached within the secure limits of any institution.

I felt very close to the founders during the Night Office. Then I sat alone in prayer asking the Father for the Spirit. It seemed (and I'll leave it at that) as if the Father moved away and I was in the presence of the founders, a clear and unmistakable presence, though they could not be described. I semed to be assessed and blest, and then the presence faded away. I do not pay a great deal of attention to this kind of thing, knowing that it is open to all sorts of illusion and unhealthy mental processes. But this I know: that God is personal, that dialogue is possible with him. For the most part, he teaches us through the medium of his silence, but on this occasion I feel that he has broken the silence and I have been reassured.

My prayer ended and I felt close to all the casualties of the Order back at a time when we badly needed reform. I am sure that they are at peace somewhere, and I am at peace. Some of the things that obsessed me have been by now largely settled—the loss of my ministry, the sense of rejection, the loss of my friends. Some other things have yet to be worked through—this enclosure, finding a new ministry, the attitude of God. There are some deep spiritual matters that have not come to any final resolution yet. I feel that they are being slowly solved, but the solution as yet evades me.

The sun is shining. It has warmed up somewhat, and there are small birds chirping in the trees. The fountain is splashing in the quadrangle, and I am enveloped in the silence. It would be good to settle down here, but that I cannot do, and neither good will nor bad will has anything to do with it.

I took my turn washing the eggs, and hummed, "May the peace

of the Lord be with you, with your friends and your family too. . . ."
Well, why not? I am developing skills, one of them being that by now
I can pick up five Jumbos in one hand. I am always happy when I
reflect that no small thing in life is ever lost, that they shall all be part
of my eternity.

Following work, I had a call from the sister in Seattle. After
much prayer and reflection on her part, she put a letter in the mail
saying "No." She knows me well enough to be able to say that I have
no talent for the work, and she is correct. Well, that takes care of my
first enthusiasm, and as for the second—slum monasticism—it has
evaporated out of my mind.

When our enthusiasms fail, and our painfully made decisions
amount to nothing, it is not a time for useless depression. The
challenge now is to discover what can be learned from the experience
so that the spiritual journey may continue.

Our mistaken enthusiasms arise, for the most part, from our
false self-image. With their failure, layer after layer of that false
image is mercilessly peeled off. The removal of each layer convinces
us of who we really are not, that is, if we patiently face up to the
reality. But who we really are begins to come into focus. This is a
purification, but it is also an enlightenment. The purpose of
transition is not to punish us for something. Its purpose is the growth
which will come when we allow these layers of false image to be
removed. Like all growth, it cannot be rushed and will not be there
until the transition reaches its final resolution. Suffering is
inseparable from the process, but it is not its essential content.

If we cling to the false image—self as the ideal person, employee,
chaplain, the just man who did not err, the misunderstood, the
underrated person—the whole process will degenerate into self-
vindication, or, worse still, into vindictiveness. If we face the failure
of our enthusiasms and the need for quick solutions, we shall find
that the reversal of our expectations brings with it some recognition
of who we are and who we are not.

I feel at this point that my purpose in the Church is inseparable
from contributing to the well-being of others. The Fathers of the
Desert would call that an illusion from the devil. I would be inclined
to say that as much growth comes from working our way through our
illusions as comes from mulling over our brilliant insights. Celtic

monasticism would have been quite happy with my less than juridical approach to the life, but the Roman passion for organizing everything helped to wipe Celtic monasticism from the map. It has taken us centuries in religious life to get back to where we are able to respond freely to the Spirit again.

I made a trip to Ogden to renew my driver's license. It was my first time out of the enclosure since my return two months previously. I was anxious to see what the experience would be like. It turned out to be less than interesting. I felt completely detached from the whole scene. What I want is something meaningful to be doing with life, not just be wandering about town. I got the license, although I failed three of the questions. I answered two of the three incorrectly by playing it safe and answering too strictly. It did not impress the officer. There were three parts in the third question; it was one of those true or false tests. As it turned out, all three were false, and I was supposed to know that. I felt that testing my knowledge through the medium of three false suggestions was quite irrational. I tried to explain to the officer that such an approach to an examination was philosophically untenable—in fact, quite unacceptable. He would not agree, and I had the distinct impression that he did not grasp the subtlety of the point. He took the stance of those who feel that being in control imparts wisdom, although his thoughts were as fluid as the bowel of an anchorite.

The friend who keeps my life organized called. She is going to get in touch with a House of Prayer in Seattle. She has some notion that they need a priest on the staff. If they say "Yes," I shall leave here. That might well be a mistake, and that thought might well be a pessimism originating in a lack of faith.

Needing to feel more positive about things, I sought out a man in the community for advice. I got taken over the coals for analyzing too much, and for not being simple. I told him that I was not, indeed, a simple soul, that the house was full of them, and that they didn't know a damn thing about what was going on in the lives of those around them. I told him that if I found God again in the closeness of his friendship, I might find some measure of simplicity. I said that simplicity will come with the worth God himself will have created in me. I have no desire to return to image seeking. I want to know what

65

manner of God this is who cares enough about us to be crucified for it. In the meantime, I told him, my analyzing helps me in small part to be aware of the problems of others from studying the structures of my own.

He could not understand that God could be a problem. Most people, he said, had no problem with God. Cheers for your enclosure, I thought to myself. It seems to me that people who have no problem with God, people who say, "God? Oh sure, everybody knows about God," have not a notion of the profundity of the mystery. If our god is a warm, comfortable self-assurance, there is indeed no problem. But when God takes our search seriously, when he tries to get through our egotistical barriers with some measure of real truth, the affair is something else. When he takes up the scalpel and says, "Sorry, no anesthetic," one is inclined to become a trifle analytical. In a time of transition the purpose of prayer and reflection is not to anesthetize oneself so as to remove the pain. We pray so as to lift the problem and its pain up to a higher level where it ceases to be destructive. Through prayer, reflection, and analysis, we are able to bring unconscious destructive forces to the surface and deal with them. They empower us to let go of the false layers of self-image and of the mistaken enthusiasms. The entire problem will solve itself in time when we stop fighting it.

It snowed again, and the world is a winter wonderland, the bright sun radiant through snow covered branches. Birds are singing, and there is hot coffee; it warms the heart. It is prayer, for it is with the world that God gives himself—this, my body—not with the mind alone. The tender and gentling element is the body. Even when the mind is cold and invulnerable, the body is always vulnerable. That is what makes the spiritual journey of transition possible, and it is a blessing.

Days fade away into night, and nights pale into further days as I wait to hear from the Prayer House in Seattle. There are few breaches of the routine in the enclosed life. But we had one moment of Spanish fly: somebody left the door to the cloister unlocked and two Filipinos wandered in, accosting the monks and wanting to buy candles. The cloister is off limits for women; in the old days its invasion would have been cause for excommunication, and the memory lingers. I came on the scene and ushered them out with polite insistence, but not before a minor official came by in a rush, incoherently muttering and flailing his arms. It was not a good morning.

I have been reading something insightful in Kierkegaard who was deep into depression. He said, basically, that we do not despair because we are unable to *have* something, but that in *not* having it we cannot endure being merely who we are. So it isn't the loss of the job, or the person, or the mobility, or the possessions that defeat us. It is being left alone with our empty selves. When the layers of false image have been peeled off, we have nothing to hang on to. Our egotistical image is destroyed, and we have to be satisfied to be merely ourselves. It is difficult. But a psychological death must precede every resurrection in our lives. Each time we let go of a person, a place, or even a false image, we die a little or a lot. We endure a great deal of stress. But the journey holds within itself a change of attitude, and the possibility of a real resurrection.

I do not even ask if there is a resurrection in my life. When I sit in the dark at night, or in the next day's dawn, and have little thought of God, only that he is, I pray for all who are in transition. I know that something in myself is coming to an end. I find it difficult to write anymore. It is drying up. I sometimes sit with my arm on my desk and my head on my arms. I am weary of it all. I think of my past crusades against all that I considered phony and hypocritical. I was, for the most part, wrong. I was arrogant. People need to protect themselves. The apparently strong ones, the ones who are never wrong, are very often the weakest. They need the mask, the phony front, to be secure. When we strip that away, they have nothing. None of us can afford to have our mask stripped off except to the extent that our meaning is God.

Lord, the poor who are always with us are ourselves, all of us. Teach us to gentle our feelings toward each other, to let the false masks remain lest we see our true selves and despair. Lord, I have torn too many masks from too many people, and all in the name of truth. But all that is true is not always kind, nor is my truth yours. I have much need of repentance.

12. Start to Return: Resolution

Facts lead to further facts, experiences to new experiences. One question leads to another until the fabric of our being moves outward toward the infinite, the questioner transcending all that can be called in question. Inquest or end quest, it must end somewhere.

The novice master surprised us with an insightful homily on the salt of the earth and the light of the world. What I understood him to say was that unless we grasp the truth (salt) experientially, that is, be the truth, we shall never be able to make it understandable to others. And unless it makes us cheerful inside (light), a joy reflected in our faces, we shall never make it acceptable to others.

I thought of my many friends who had the power to radiate that truth and joy to me: Christ as truth, Christ loving, Christ rising out of dying. I feel humbled by those friendships. A friendship is of very little depth unless it reveals to us how unworthy we are of it. These friends love and let be. It is their way of life. They support without directing, encourage without insisting, correct without losing their sense of humor.

To grasp with cheerfulness the mystery of God is the reward of all our struggles. The freedom of God with his truth and our freedom with risk come together with unpredictable results. What we need is a receptive spirit. Transition gouges out that receptivity in us. Yet, our spirit at any given time can receive only so much. I feel that what is meant by not being tempted beyond our strength in the journey of life is that God eases up lest his love kill us with his creative power. And since life has no meaning if God is not making the gift of himself to us, he never eases up until we are exhausted.

Coming to terms with a God of Mystery can only be expressed paradoxically. When transition has peeled off some of the false layers of our self-understanding, we come to experience a closer presence of God. It works this way: the immediacy of his presence is realized in the immediacy of our "selves" to ourselves. We begin to bypass the images and symbols, the God of our childishness. Look at it this way: the "myself" that I talk about is only a symbol, a projected image in words. If we drop this, there is only the silence of being; there is no longer a division between the "I" and the projected image: myself. Somewhat in that same way, there is no division between God who is present and the self which experiences him. He is no symbol. One cannot grasp it directly; should we try to do so it vanishes, for then what we are doing is focusing, and thus getting in the way of the reality of simply being in presence. His being is in ours and we must respect the reality and silence of being. Symbols are not now permitted. Transition cleanses away much of what prevents us being present to our own immediacy, but being present there without image, concept or self-illusion, we find ourselves present to God who is in us.

As for the rest in one's experience, the labels that people pin on us—Irish, male, priest, monk, writer and so on—are garbage. That is not who we are. We may never focus on any one element such as those mentioned, not even on adopting a contemplative stance, since to do so is to fragment the world and distort it. Each reality is linked into the all, and can be known as true only within the all. One gazes and sees All. There is no label now which will define us, other than ourselves in the self of God, one spirit with him. This is our freedom, God immediate to our immediacy—that is all. "I will be with you."

I have had a call from the House of Prayer in Seattle. They asked me to come. I shall go there wondering if it will mean the end of my transition. My bus leaves from Ogden at 6:25 A.M. Nick will drive into town. He is sorry to see me going. I am sorry to be parting from him. I have settled some things. I have come to accept the reality of these men here. I see clearly the transcendent witness of their faith. I have made my inner peace with them. Most of them make no claims at all to being anything other than men of faith, Christian farmers who take their Christianity and their farming very seriously. I like that. I have come to a deeper and more sympathetic understanding of them. For now, I have to move on. God is not fully revealed in anything of human founding, this God who breaks and mends human hearts.

I spent four months in Seattle. Very little was happening. My unsalaried services were not even enough to warrant my continuing to receive room and board, though there were a few good things— prayer-days, conferences, retreats.

My contemplative friend visited and we spent a day by the water on Vashon Island in the Sound. We looked at pebbles polished by the sea, and at the "secret rainbows on the domes of deep sea shells" (Jeffers). We talked about God ("What do you mean, he?" she asked), and she recommended a few books which might be helpful ("I hate pious talk"). Mostly, I sat there and cursed my fate for having made a decision that did not work out. She introduced me to Joan, a friend of hers who had herself been through transition, and is now all heart. Joan assured me that I had done the proper thing, that people in transition usually try a few things before settling down, that it is a legitimate part of the process. She had done so. I felt strengthened by both of them.

There were a couple of other insightful moments which contributed to bringing the transition to its resolution. The first had to do with friendship. I came to realize deep within myself that the friendships of celibates, for all their real necessity, are not an end in themselves; their end is God. He originates them; he is their ultimate purpose.

Christ tells us that he no longer calls us servants; he calls us friends. But to know the friendship of Christ, one must first of all have experienced human friendship. We have to be true to that friendship and not let our fidelity wander when it seems lost— friendship being a task as well as a reward. We have to see constantly the reflection of Christ in the eyes of our friends, both his humanity and his divinity. In them we see our beatitude in sacramental form. Our way to salvation is made much easier if we are faithful to them. They, in turn, must make our gaze go past themselves to God. They are only the image of what God's love will perfect. My friends will never go begging for my friendship, but I do not stop there. They are the many facets of the love of God. They are sacred to me, and have shown me something of beatitude. God's love is flawless, but I did not know its blessedness until I knew my friends.

The second insightful moment came on a day on which it was indicated to me that I should move on. I was in a state of panic. I had no place to go to. I had prayed for hours and had come to the acceptance of the fact that there was nothing for me to do but to return to the abbey. I called one of my friends long distance, the one who taught me that love was a community builder. She panicked and began shouting on the phone, "You can't go back there! You can't go back!"

When I hung up, I decided to walk into the city center because walking is therapeutic when we are under stress. Each step of the way I beat God over the head with my thoughts and prayers. When I got down to Woolworth's on 3rd Street, I took the bus back. Three blind men carrying canes got on at 8th and Pine. They sat together on a side seat reserved for the handicapped and laughed and talked about God and about a friend of theirs who was to be baptized that night in their church. It was then that, in some strange way, I saw God as Trinity giving the totality of himself to me in love, a love that judged me for being the blind one. We were at the corner of Broadway and Pike.

I realized, on reflection, that I had been unconsciously of the opinion that a great experience of God would surely be had within a correspondingly great event. Now I know that God gives the totality of himself even in the littlest of things, even in nothing at all. He simply gives, and we are too blind to see it. I was stunned by his generosity. I had been inhibited because I had been seeing so much that was of no concern to God. The three blind men were uninhibited because their inner vision was intact.

I got back to the Prayer House, and that night dreamt of the Trinity whose reproach to me was, "You are not joining in the music." When I awoke I knew that I would have to be part of the music of life, putting anxiety behind me. Shortly after that, I had a letter from the friend who helps me be organized. She had come across an ad in the National Catholic Reporter from a priory in the midwest. They were looking for a chaplain. I applied for the position, and was hired for a year.

As my writing comes to a close, I am back in ministry to people again. My transition is very much at an end. The nature of the resolution, however, is not quite what I had anticipated. I realize now that it does not consist in straightening out the outer events of our lives. It is the end, for now, of a spiritual journey. It does not consist in finding a place where we might settle down. It does not consist in being with friends. It is more than any meaningful ministry. Those are things for which we long. It is more. It consists in making an inner peace with God, with ourselves and with the future.

We discover that God will be God, irrespective of what we do or think. We come to know that he is not merely the object of our thoughts, but the subject of a personal encounter. This encounter, however, is had on his terms. We come to know that he is concrete and actual, and not merely the abstraction of wishful thinkers. He, the living one to whom we speak, or before whom we are silent, has claims on us. We cease trying to control him. His ways are not ours, so we let him be. For my own part, when I stand at the altar and recall into the present his own transition through time and space and personal passion, all times and places become one in the togetherness of his body. More than ever, I share the priesthood of all the people who consecrate this togetherness.

We make peace with ourselves and with others, flaws and feet of clay notwithstanding. All of us in transition were caught in a paradox, trapped in finite worries while hungering for an absolute, feeling rejected and worthless while longing to be of some value to others. It was this sense of futility which caused all the anguish. The resolution of our transition is had when the anguish tears away some of the false self-image, the myths and the expectations, the arrogance, and restores reality to us. That reality is the experience of a whole new inner freedom.

But reality is not something which is simply possessed. It has to be interpreted. It becomes the place of either our despair or our hope. If we do not hold to a faith which gives assurance that the transcendence of time and space, of all that seems lost, is possible, a faith that offers the fullness of life and the divine to us, there is nothing for it but to see existence as absurd, and to despair. But with faith it is possible to see that reality, irrespective of its limitations, is the place where God gives the gift of himself, where mercy, grace and personal purpose are found. The resolution of transition, or the end of the spiritual journey for now, is found in a faith and freedom which transfigure and ennoble the meaning of reality, making it the place where we find God.

72

The death we die in parting from friends and places, from all that is comforting and familiar, from all we had planned for the future, is not a dead end. We have died into those friends, places and events. No moment of goodness, nothing that has ever been loved, is ever ultimately lost. The apparent losing is the process of a gradual resurrection. We are not trapped at all. The relationships we have established to people and places will one day reveal our personal presence in them. The personal in us is no longer confined entirely to a physical body. It is growing and rising and spreading out, as we give the entirety of ourselves now here, now there, now to this person, now to that.

My own transition is ended because now I experience that nobody and nothing is lost. As an organism, I am within this small bit of space and time, but as a spirit person I live on in my friends and in the places I love. I know that my reality is a gradual dying into resurrection, and already I sense the beginning of a life that will be universal because of loving. I grasp it now in faith and partial vision. I have experienced something; I have not merely invented it. Something has been disclosed to me: that living is inseparable from loving, that friendship is divine, immortal, transcending time, and space, and loss. For that reason I have made peace with the future. The future is the place where rising out of dying will continue. The only future I care to know is not something temporal; it is God coming toward me. The thoughts that caused pain and panic are put to rest. The transition is ended.

For now, at least, there is an abiding God whose continued reticence is eloquent of acceptance. And life, and love, and my friends are celebrating a new togetherness in the deeps of my heart.